T0208323

# MAXIMIZED

## Prevailing Over
## My **Bipolar Depression**

### MAXIMILLIAN STANGARONE

**BALBOA**
PRESS
A DIVISION OF HAY HOUSE

Balboa Press books may be ordered through booksellers or by contacting:

Balboa Press
A Division of Hay House
1663 Liberty Drive
Bloomington, IN 47403
www.balboapress.com
1 (877) 407-4847

Because of the dynamic nature of the Internet, any web addresses or
links contained in this book may have changed since publication and
may no longer be valid. The views expressed in this work are solely those
of the author and do not necessarily reflect the views of the publisher,
and the publisher hereby disclaims any responsibility for them.

The author of this book does not dispense medical advice or prescribe the use
of any technique as a form of treatment for physical, emotional, or medical
problems without the advice of a physician, either directly or indirectly. The
intent of the author is only to offer information of a general nature to help
you in your quest for emotional and spiritual well-being. In the event you use
any of the information in this book for yourself, which is your constitutional
right, the author and the publisher assume no responsibility for your actions.

Any people depicted in stock imagery provided by Getty Images are
models, and such images are being used for illustrative purposes only.
Certain stock imagery © Getty Images.

Print information available on the last page.

ISBN: 978-1-9822-3060-9 (sc)
ISBN: 978-1-9822-3061-6 (hc)
ISBN: 978-1-9822-3062-3 (e)

Library of Congress Control Number: 2019908878

Balboa Press rev. date: 08/16/2019

# Dedication

This book is dedicated to my grandparents, Umberto and Costanza Stangarone, Massimiliano and Angela Tassielli, and to my parents Vito and Mary Stangarone, Italian immigrants who came to this country with nothing but the ideals of faith, hope, love, hard work, and sacrifice for themselves and for future generations.

Secondly, for the happiness and prosperity for future generations of our family—Dean, Alex, Jack, Abby, and Charlie.

# Contents

# Introduction

My bipolar depression was difficult to overcome. It took me fourteen years and numerous trials and solutions, which added up to effectively managing my illness. It was like traveling without a guide or a map and there was no one there to show me the way. But I had an innate faith that all would work itself out, and the determination to carry out my faith.

I endured severe depression and multiple manic episodes, and came out victorious over my illness, achieving a strong and healthy state of existence, and I believe anyone can. There were many components that contributed to my well-being and helped me overcome the hurdles in my path.

A deep and painful depression that lasted four and a half years left me labeled as "medication resistant," and with little hope. It was at that time that my doctor recommended an alternative to medication. She believed Electroconvulsive Therapy (ECT) treatments were my next best course of action. ECT is a procedure where a patient is administered an electrical current to induce a seizure, which can provide relief from suffering for those afflicted with mental disorders. I had ECT treatments for a year and a half, three times per week, with partial success. It lifted me out of my deep depression into a more moderate one.

The next course of action was to retry medications, as my mood had been somewhat elevated. Unfortunately, medications that previously had no effect on me would now send me into a manic episode. Once that mania was resolved, I would return to my previous moderate depression. This phase of my illness lasted another eight years, until I came upon a newer medication, a mood stabilizer. This medication took me the rest of the way out of my depression.

I achieved stability with great effort, along with much trial and error. Once stable, the after-effects of the illness left me with little confidence and a great deal of anxiety. It took me seven more years of work with a therapist to take the necessary steps to rebuild my confidence and strength in order to become healthier and happier than I was before the onset of this illness.

Being free of setbacks from depression for the past eight years has given me much reason for hope moving forward. Through great effort in effectively managing my symptoms, such as reading, writing, being my own advocate, exercise, proper diet, therapy, meditation, prayer, and relying on my external supports, I succeeded in the restoration of my health—and I believe everyone can succeed. But you must be willing to fight this illness, to persevere through your difficulties and whatever setbacks you may have. You will come out on top a better and stronger individual.

To those of you out there suffering from depression or bipolar disorder, I hope this book will be helpful to you. I was given hope, inspiration, and encouragement along the way and it is my hope that I can give this to you. The biggest lesson I learned is perseverance. Don't give up. Don't ever give up!

"Our greatest glory is not in never falling,
but in rising every time we fall."
—Confucius

# CHAPTER 1

## My Story

My bipolar illness first manifested itself in the spring of 1983. I was preparing to graduate from college at the State University of New York at Albany with a bachelor's degree. I was twenty-one years old. One month was left in my final semester and my thoughts, which previously focused on the day-to-day affairs of school, classes, studying, relationships, social life, now turned toward the future.

Some of my friends knew what their next step was, while some, like myself, had no concrete idea. A couple of them were planning to go to medical school, another into the accounting field, and another to continue to graduate school to become a teacher. I never gave it much thought. I truly was living in a bubble, living a day at a time, enjoying my life at college.

I was graduating with an economics degree and a minor

in business administration. Albany was known for its business school. For practicality, I decided to study economics rather than follow my intuition and seek out my passions in psychology and the sciences. I did, however, take numerous psychology courses; this was an area of study that I sought out during my teen years, and I continue to read about psychology as an adult.

Choosing the conventional business route was a mistake, but such mistakes were all part of the learning process. As I began to ponder the bigger questions in life, I became a little unglued. I had an idea about what I wanted to do with my life—I vaguely thought that I would enter the medical profession in some capacity. However, due to my lack of belief in myself, I dismissed this notion because I felt I wouldn't measure up to the other students.

This lack of confidence stayed with me until my late twenties, when I addressed this issue with Dr. Flo Rosof, a licensed social worker whom I decided to see to discuss my issues of inadequacy and occupational direction. She instilled in me the idea of taking risks, such as entering the medical field as a radiologic technologist. I will share more about my work with Dr. Rosof in the chapter on therapy.

Being unsure about who I was and what my direction would be became a little overwhelming. Rather than talk about what I was feeling with friends, I kept my thoughts and feelings to myself, and slowly and steadily built up fear and anxiety about my future. As time wore on, I became quiet and withdrawn.

April arrived and graduation was upon me. Aware of the fear that was growing within me on a daily basis, I started feeling paranoid. I felt that people around me had suspect motives and that they were out to get me. I did not understand what was going on, but these feelings grew on a daily basis. All the while, I kept this inside me and I was terrified of the consequences if I spoke aloud to anyone. As the days wore on, I thought that every stranger I encountered wanted to harm me. My world became black and white. People either were good or evil.

As this terror became worse in subsequent days, I could not rest, eat, or sleep. I began believing that Bruce Springsteen was God, and this took me further into my psychosis. His song lyrics filled my mind. In my current state of mind through his music, heaven as well as hell dwelled within me. His lyrics from "Promised Land" led me to believe that heaven was here on earth. My "mission" was to follow Bruce (God in my current state of mind). I took the lyrics in his songs literally. In the song, "Saint in the City," he claimed he was a prophet. I believed it. I believed every word in his songs. In the song "Badlands," he sang of living every day on this earth and rising above this world, this "hell" of a world. The fear was insufferable yet I did not tell a soul.

On the outside, I was quiet; on the inside, I trembled with fear.

I mistrusted most every person I came in contact with, with the exception of my roommates. At this point, I didn't care about my appearance, hadn't slept for a week, and stayed in my room listening to Springsteen's songs over and over. One day I felt the need to go outside. I began walking outside without shoes or socks. One of my friends noticed me walking barefoot and he knew he had to do something. My abnormal behavior was, he told me later, something he had experienced with a relative of his. His aunt had a mental illness. He immediately alerted my parents.

My parents came up quickly from Long Island. I was subsequently admitted to a hospital in Albany and stayed there for a week. I was like a zombie from all of the medications that they administered. I was then brought back home to East Northport, and there was admitted to Huntington Hospital where medications of Haldol (an atypical antipsychotic) and lithium (a mood stabilizer) were given to me. After a couple of weeks, I returned to normal and was sent home. It was a scary episode and I felt relieved to move beyond that awful experience.

I was diagnosed with bipolar disorder. Bipolar disorder, also known as manic-depressive illness, is a chemical imbalance in the brain that causes abnormal shifts in mood, energy, and activity for a persistent period of time. The illness leads to a significant disturbance in the ability to carry out day-to-day tasks and can require the intervention of a medical professional or hospitalization in a psychiatric facility. My disorder was further complicated by psychosis experienced as a break from reality—for example, that Bruce Springsteen was God.

The doctor who treated me at Huntington Hospital went on to be my psychiatrist for the next thirteen years. Dr. Lajpat Gandhi was a wise and soft-spoken psychiatrist from India. He had a thick accent and a very gentle manner. I would see Dr. Gandhi on a monthly basis until I felt my "mentally ill days" were far behind me. Dr. Gandhi was warm, compassionate, and kind. Over time I came to trust him. He would always tell me to cherish my health, and while I did, I now have the capacity to understand his message with a combination of therapy and lithium as an older, more mature adult.

After becoming mentally stable, I came to the conclusion that the real world wasn't so scary. Realizing that any job was a good place to start, Charlie, a good friend of mine from college, gave me my first opportunity. His father was a regional manager for Dolly Madison Ice Cream Company, so I began my career as a sales representative for the company (unfortunately, they are no longer in business). As a sales rep I visited supermarkets in Suffolk County, making sure the products were well represented and marketed correctly, and I served as a liaison between the company and the managers in all of these supermarkets. There was a regular regional contest for selling the most cases of ice cream. I welcomed the challenge and actually won a TV set. This gave my spirits a much needed lift, as I was still getting acclimated to the real world.

At this point, it was two years after my initial diagnosis and

I had finally found my footing. In 1985, I started working as an accounting clerk. After a year, I was promoted to accountant, a position I retained for a few years. I continued taking lithium during this time.

In 1992, I decided to go back to school and obtain a second bachelor's degree in medical biology with a concentration in radiologic technology at Long Island University in Brookville, Long Island. School and learning were always comfortable and exciting for me. When it came to science and psychology, I was passionate and enthusiastic, and absorbed material like a sponge. The clinical aspect, however, was foreign to me. It was very technical, but I managed to get through it. I managed B's and A's in my classes, but C's in the clinical portion of the program. While I was fulfilling my prerequisite classes, I worked at Chemical Bank as an administrative assistant. However, I still questioned my diagnosis. After three to four years of stability, I felt as though I was okay and that the problems around the time of my college graduation were just a bump in the road. I was okay now, was steady, had a stable job for a few years, and showed no signs of my illness. This led me to think that perhaps lack of a belief in myself contributed to my symptoms. I thought that up until age 21 I was fine, so it seemed that two years after the manic episodes I was fine again. Perhaps it was the stigma associated with this illness. It was then that I decided to look for more answers as I wondered if my diagnosis was correct.

It was recommended that I try the Mayo Clinic in Minnesota. I was free of any symptoms for five years. Was there really something wrong with me? After a week of various testing, it was confirmed. Like it or not, it was confirmed that I had bipolar disorder 1.

At the young age of 21, I allowed the illness to define who I was, and on top of that, I thought it was more of a character flaw than a chemical imbalance in the brain. I told myself no more questioning and that this was something I had to live with. At least that's what I thought at the time.

After completing my second bachelor's degree, I worked as a radiologic technologist at St. Claire's Hospital in Manhattan from 1994 to 1998. In a nutshell, I felt great. I had a busy social life as well. I made a couple of good friends at the hospital, went out on weekends, and started a softball team called the St. Claire Saints. We played our games in Central Park and came in second place one year. It was a co-ed team and we went out after most games. It was a great way to socialize and meet people in the hospital. (I still love playing softball to this day, though I am not quite at the level I was at in my thirties, when I was in my prime.) But it was the most enjoyable social activity for me.

In 1996, I decided to stop taking lithium; it had been over ten years since I had had any setbacks or any symptoms of my illness. I was overconfident in my thinking. As it turned out, it was a bad decision. Two years subsequent to the ceasing of my medication, I was laid off at the hospital and it triggered a major depressive episode from which I did not recover from for fourteen years.

I fell deep into the depression hard and fast. It was no more than two weeks into my downward spiral that I was in a hellish nightmare. The first two weeks I was still living in my apartment in Brooklyn, but I then moved to my parents' home on Long Island where I lived for several years. Those first four and a half years were painful, lonely, and at times, almost unendurable. I barely uttered a word, spent my days lying on my couch, and basically withstood my unrelenting pain. Initially, I didn't know what hit me. I just knew something was wrong—deeply wrong with me. I felt like I had been run over by a bus. I was dead in many aspects—my mind ceased functioning. I could not take care of myself.

In going back to live with my family they all pitched in and tended to my situation. First things first—I needed to get to a doctor, specifically a psychiatrist, right away. I suffered greatly during this period and was disheartened along the way, as numerous doctors and medications were tried without success.

During this time, I dreaded any and all contact with people. I was afraid to go outside. I felt paralyzed if I ran into anyone who tried talking to me. I remember one instance when I went to a fair with my mother and sisters. I ran into an old friend, Dom. As he approached me, my fear and anxiety levels overwhelmed me. I was unable to process any information. Fear raced through my mind and my heart, which was beating fast and loud. As he spoke, I put on a face of understanding, nodding my head up and down in typical social rituals. I found it difficult to speak, managing a "Hi Dom," and then retreated back into my inner world, which included head pain and a fear-filled heart. Aside from my condition not allowing me to process information, my fears enveloped me as he spoke and I could not utter much in return. He continued talking, but when he saw I was unable to respond, he turned to my sister. She took him aside and explained my condition.

On another occasion, I went to my uncle and aunt's new home for the first time, and the daily paralyzing fear gripped me while I was with them. They showed me around their apartment and as was the case with Dom, I couldn't comprehend anything they were saying. I just wanted to be home on my couch away from contact with other people.

As time wore on and my hopes dimmed, my only relief came when I slept. After sleeping for eight to ten hours, the pain and all that went with it would resume again for the next fourteen to sixteen hours. It felt like this cycle would last forever.

I tried dozens of medications of all types (mostly antidepressants and mood stabilizers), all without any effect. I remained the same. On the one hand, my depressive period of 14 years felt like an eternity but there also was another feeling—from within or somewhere up above—or both—that made me continue on. This indefinable feeling made me want to go on one more day.

My family was my backbone. I am one of six children. I have two older siblings, Umberto (Burt) and Constance (Connie). There were three more after me—Angela and Susanne, twins born in 1963, and Martin, born in 1968.

Aside from my family, two other things helped me get through each day: reading and writing. I don't know why I started to write, but I did. And when I could, I read anything that inspired me.

Since the beginning of the depression something within me, call it faith or sheer will, told me I would not be beaten. This early attitude was that of a fighter, and my perseverance up to this point helped me to face my current challenge in life.

Early on I began writing on a legal pad daily, sometimes just a word or phrase like, "hang in there" or "I'll get there." I wrote mostly for encouragement; from this I learned two things: writing would help me immensely along the way and would give me hope.

And I read what I could. There was one author, William Styron, who wrote *Darkness Visible*, his memoir of his depression. No other author has conveyed what this dark period was like for me better than Mr. Styron.

In his book, he poignantly described his depression. He states on page 58, "I had now reached that phase of the disorder where all sense of hope had vanished, along with the idea of a futurity; my brain had become less an organ of thought than an instrument registering minute by minute, varying degrees of its own suffering." On page 62 he goes on to state, "The pain is unrelenting, and what makes the condition intolerable is the foreknowledge that no remedy will come—not in a day, an hour, a month, or a minute. If there is mild relief, one knows that it is only temporary; more pain will follow. It is hopelessness even more than the pain that crushes the soul.

"So, the decision-making of daily life involves not, as in normal affairs, shifting from one annoying situation to another less annoying—or from discomfort to relative comfort, or from boredom to activity, but moving from pain to pain. One does not abandon, even briefly, one's bed of nails, but is attached to it wherever one goes. And this results in a striking experience— one which I have called, borrowing military terminology, the situation of the walking wounded. For in virtually any other serious sickness, a patient who felt similar devastation would be lying flat in bed, possibly sedated and hooked up to the tubes and wires of life-support systems, but at the very least in a pasture of repose and in an isolated setting. His invalidism would be necessary, unquestioned, and honorably attained. However, the sufferer from depression has no such option and therefore finds himself, like a walking casualty of war, thrust into the most intolerable social and family situations. There he must, despite the anguish devouring his brain, present a face approximating the one that is associated with ordinary events and companionship. He must try to utter small talk, and be responsive to questions, and knowingly nod and frown and, God help him, even smile. But it is a fierce trial attempting to speak a few simple words."

His words spoke to me on a very deep level. My pain was as unrelenting as his was. My brain also recorded my suffering. But I was not alone. William Styron summarized in one paragraph what I had been feeling for over four years. I'd found someone who understood me, who had gone through what I now was going through, and more importantly, he had come out of his nightmare to a better place. Yes, I told myself, if he can get through this, then so can I.

On to more doctors and more trials of medications, until one doctor finally declared that I was medication resistant. But not to worry, she said calmly—there were alternative treatments out there. So on to my next trial; Electroconvulsive Therapy Treatments (ECT). This is a procedure in which electric currents are passed through the brain, intentionally triggering a brief seizure. Its aim is to change brain chemistry. This will be discussed in the chapter on treatments. At this point I was willing to try anything to get relief from these unbearably painful symptoms.

My parents took me to St. Catherine's Hospital in Smithtown, NY, three times a week for one and a half years, in search of a treatment for my depression. These treatments were my last hope in pulling out of this hellish major depressive episode. It felt like the only solution since I was told that I was medication resistant. It was on the way to and from these treatments that I often thought, "Is this really happening?" It was a nightmare come true.

I remember my treatments very clearly. I would sit in a waiting room with great anxiety, but also patiently listening for my name to be called. There were always one or two other patients in the room with me, some seemingly normal individuals and others, very despondent. I recall an elderly priest who was unresponsive to anyone around him, he was in a catatonic state.

When the nurse called my name, I would enter a small room where my psychiatrist, a nurse, and an anesthesiologist waited. I was directed to a chair, and electrodes were attached to my temples. The anesthesiologist administered a sedative through an IV, which would cause me to become unconscious. While asleep, a brief seizure was induced via electrodes and I would wake up several minutes later, unaware of the procedure that had taken place.

As the months wore on, I began to emerge groggy and disoriented. My brain was getting foggy after these treatments. I would only have a few more treatments after this one, because my doctor decided it was in my best interest to stop ECT to avoid future harm. Most of the year and a half of these treatments have been washed away from my memory. This was a big side effect of this procedure.

The ECT treatments were partially successful, taking me from a deep depression into a more moderate one. I was no longer suffering to the extent that I had been, but I still had a difficult time processing information. In one case I vividly remember my brother Burt asking me what I was experiencing while I was watching the news. I said, "All I see are two people speaking to each other back and forth without understanding what they are saying."

After six years, I had some hope that a medication would now have an effect on me. As I emerged from my first four and a half years of darkness, and after my one and a half years of ECT treatments, what was next?

It was my hope that a medication could take over and pull me all the way out of depression. Unfortunately, it would take eight more years of drug experimentation until I thankfully found a medication that worked for me.

It was a long fourteen years and took a big chapter of my life, as I was 36 years of age when it began and 51 when I found the right combination of medication, treatments, and therapy. Exercise, reading, journal writing, prayer, and meditation also helped immensely. I had a "never give up" attitude and the unconditional support of my family, which helped me to become a stronger and healthier individual.

After my ECT treatments were over, I began working for my brother, Martin, whose beverage store had just opened. I was able to function as a cashier and did a lot of physical work, lifting cases and kegs of beer for deliveries. I tried to pull myself out of the lingering depression with the help of work and positive thinking. In my mind, I had taken a big step—functioning, even though it was in a limited capacity.

Though I didn't know it at the time, St. James Beverage was a great place for me to be. In addition to spending time with my brother Martin, I also had the support of my four other siblings. My oldest brother, Burt, introduced me to one of my first books on the subject of depression, *Win the Battle* by Bob Olson. In this book, Olson recalls his five-year battle with depression.

He contemplated taking his life on more than one occasion and emerged on the other side of his depression a healthy, happy man.

I want to touch on this one difficult and painful subject—suicide. If you have thoughts of suicide, seek out a professional. In the back of this book I have included crisis hotline numbers to call, or call 911, or go to the emergency room of a hospital. There are many people who have contemplated taking their own lives during times of crisis. Seek help and right your ship again. Don't become a statistic. Never quit. Persevere and reach out to anyone you can, be it a loved one, a healthcare professional, or a clergyman—or find a friend or support group. Believe me, it's all worth it in the end to have your health, peace of mind, and happiness back.

I was, however, hospitalized several times for my mania. My hospital stays were typically one to three weeks. I was immediately given antipsychotic medications that were heavily sedating. I slept a good deal of the time. Otherwise, I would simply pace back and forth within the unit (a side effect of one of my medications). Many of the patients there were like me, quiet and alone. I didn't participate in any type of group functions and kept to myself, patiently waiting for the medications to eliminate the terror that dwelled in my mind for several days at a time during my visits.

I recall one night at the beginning of a manic episode (all my manic episodes involved psychosis) when I was seated on the couch in my parents' family room with the thought that the devil was standing outside the window. I was petrified at this notion and it stayed with me as I tried to watch TV. There was a constant state of panic in me, but I told myself to try to watch TV, that the medications would eventually take over and I would be asleep soon. This happened more than a few times during these episodes.

On another occasion during one of my manic episodes, which I do not totally recall, I drove out east to the Hamptons on Long Island. Oblivious to where I was and what time it was, I was completely lost. My parents called the police and they found me. The role of a caregiver to someone mentally ill can be difficult, and at times like this one, frightful.

One of my most vivid memories of my most unnerving episode came when there was no family around and I had to see a psychiatrist immediately. In my frantic and psychotic state, I couldn't drive. I had to take a cab and, in my current state of mind, dwelled on this unknown person—whom I feared was evil—to take me to my doctor's appointment. I was terrified the entire way there, not uttering a word. In retrospect, I realized that having family support means everything. Just this one instance without them was a nightmare.

As I've now shared with you a couple of my psychotic manic episodes, I must say that they paled in comparison to my most dreadful days of deep depression where I suffered greatly, intensely, and for a duration of four and a half years.

Once a mania was resolved, I was back at the store. I can't tell you how disheartening these episodes were, but I can tell you that I found my favorite word in the English language during this time: perseverance. I never stopped trying to find a resolution to my illness.

I remember a few times when I was at the store, hanging onto reality by a thread, as psychosis started to envelop me at the onset of a manic episode. I would be ringing up beverages and giving out change and trying to stay rooted in reality. The level of fear and mistrust of others would escalate to a terrifying level. I tried many times to hold out as long as I could at the store, but my level of distorted thinking would heighten until I had to leave for a week or so. I would then go to the psych ward of a nearby hospital where my symptoms would be quelled with medications until I recovered.

Sometimes I would go back to the store before I was ready. I somehow managed to rise every time I fell, thus the quote at the introduction to this chapter. I think this was my greatest achievement over the course of several years while at the beverage store. It's not the falling down, but the rising up each and every time we get knocked down that makes the difference.

As I look back now on all of the falls and setbacks, I think to myself that had it not been for those events, I would not have the inner strength that I do. This inner strength has enabled me to be able to handle and get through all of these circumstances. I have become more knowledgeable about myself, more integrated as a person and more whole with a stronger psyche than ever before.

A constant thought that kept me going was a quote from Vince Lombardi. He said, "Winning isn't everything, it's the only thing." And winning meant reclaiming my life again.

There were several side effects due to the medications I was taking, weight gain (I gained 50 pounds), nausea, vomiting, involuntary muscle twitching, and other assorted ailments. I also had irreparable damage to my kidneys due to the lithium I had taken for several years. I had to eventually stop taking this medication to avoid further harm.

My faith and my family were my backbone. I prayed in my writing. My family took me to doctors' appointments, attended seminars, comforted me, and, simply, were there for me.

I appreciated all of my brother Martin's hard work; he worked six to seven days a week, logging in ten- to twelve-hour days.

I immensely appreciated the opportunity my brother Martin gave me. Had I been doing nothing physically and mentally, it would have been difficult for me to keep a positive attitude. Being sedentary mentally and physically is not conducive to change.

You see all walks of life at the beverage store. Customers, like all people, choose to see their glass as either half empty or half full. I choose half full—it keeps me going.

Winter at the beverage store is slow. In the summer, there are many people of different walks of life buying beverages for parties and the beach. There's much banter on plans for the weekend and it's a pleasant environment. However, during the brutal winter months there are pretty much only the regulars who come in to purchase their beer quietly.

I certainly am not a psychologist, but some seem to just want an outlet in alcohol—something to get away from their problems and the drudgery of their daily lives. I've come to have more compassion for them as well and my fellow man after what I have been through. Life isn't easy for anyone. Plato, the Greek philosopher said, "Be kind, for everyone you meet is fighting a hard battle."

When I was a little more "with it," I tried to impart a little positivity into my conversations at the store, and tried to leave customers feeling better off than when they came in.

Some of the stories I heard were sad, some touching. I truly believe that if these negative addictions could be swapped for something more positive, people would feel better about themselves. For example, rather than have that six pack of beer in the evening after work, take a walk to wake up the senses. There's something to be said about getting out of your own head a little bit to appreciate the little things life has to offer, like having your health.

Coming from a place where I hadn't had my health for several years, I appreciate the gift of health more than most and I am thankful for it on a daily basis. Problems always arise, but I believe if your mind and heart are sufficiently grounded in gratitude for all the things you do have, it far—and I do mean far—outweighs the smaller problems in daily life.

Everyone has problems. But it is true that the manner in which you respond to them makes all the difference in the world.

Helen Keller said, "Although the world is full of suffering, it is also full of the overcoming of it."

Finally, after eight years of working at my brother's store I went back to Dr. Marianne Hendrix, the doctor who recommended ECT treatments. This time she saw I was in a better place than I had been nine years earlier. She told me that all of the antidepressants I was taking with no success were probably never going to get me healthy. So in the spring of 2012, she started me on a new medication called Abilify, a mood stabilizer, and slowly but surely as she increased the dosage, it worked for me! After a couple of months I achieved stability for the first time in fourteen years! I was cautious at first, but as the months wore on I became more hopeful and optimistic. It would still take me an additional five years to completely feel like myself again because I had a great deal of anxiety to work through and I had lost all confidence in myself. This is where my psychologist came in to really pull me the rest of the way out to a healthier, more balanced life. These professionals are here so that if I were to have any setbacks they can be caught early, minimizing their severity and duration.

So, twenty years later, after all those ECT treatments, after all the doctors I saw, the dozens of medications I tried, after all the disheartening setbacks I had, I had now found a peaceful state of mind.

To anyone out there struggling with depression or bipolar depression, there are new medications and treatments coming out all of the time. Modern science is making great strides in the treatment of mental illness and they will continue to do so. I know about unendurable levels of suffering, but don't give up—never give up!

I thank God for my makeup, that I am a fighter and that I never gave up. I thank God for my family and all of their support.

I also now have an excellent therapist and psychiatrist—very important. It took me almost 5 years to gain back my confidence and spirit, though I am stronger and better for having overcome adversity.

Through my most difficult times I looked to my grandfather, Massimiliano Tassielli. Both he and my grandmother, Angela Tassielli, endured the greatest of hardships and poverty. They lost three children to typhoid, which was rampant in Europe in the 1920s and 1930s. But Massimiliano had in his mind that he would make a better life for himself and his family. He also had in mind a better outcome for my brothers and sisters and their children as well. So he stowed away on a ship to America. He came with nothing but faith in God, hope for the future, and love for his family. He worked hard, made sacrifices, and was determined to make his dreams a reality—ideals that make America great. Massimiliano's story is one of courage and hope.

He is truly the greatest and strongest man that I've ever encountered. So as much as you can be hopeful. Perseverance and determination are the best remedies that I have found. In the immortal words of Jim Valvano, a courageous basketball coach who bravely battled cancer to the end... "Don't give up, don't ever give up!"

## My Roots

I didn't know it then but my childhood and adolescence, which were filled with a mixture of love, nurturing, faith, and trials, would serve to carry me through my most difficult and trying times as an adult.

My beginnings were very modest. I was born on May 1, 1961, at Metropolitan Hospital in Manhattan, New York, to Italian immigrants Vito and Mary Stangarone. I was ultimately one of six children

Burt, my older brother, is a self-made man. He started working at the age of 12 delivering newspapers. He also worked for our neighbor restoring ovens. He later worked as a pizza man for my father, then upon graduation from college became a successful bond trader on Wall Street in Manhattan. He is most proud of his family; he is a father to two fine young men, Dean and Alex. He attributes his success to the value of hard work that our family instilled in him, and appreciation of the adopted country of our parents and grandparents.

My older sister, Connie, is a school social worker and lives with her husband Greg, in Brooklyn, New York. Her biggest motivation comes from helping others. She fondly recalls our childhood years when we lived with our devoted grandparents in Astoria, New York. She is also a generous aunt, daughter, and sister.

Two years after Connie, I arrived. Like my grandfather I am a good, strong, and determined man.

Of my two twin sisters, Susanne, is the most creative of the family, while Angela, the other twin, is the most intelligent. Susanne works as a career advisor at a university in Manhattan and resides in New Jersey with her husband Robert and son Jack, whom she considers her greatest success. Her fondest recollection of growing up in Astoria was that our family was part of a village, we had an abundance of friends and family always coming and going. We would spend our days playing out in the street with numerous friends. In contrast, after moving to the suburbs of Long Island, we all found it isolating and a bit lonely.

Angela works as a research coordinator at a big hospital in Manhattan and resides on the upper west side. Her strongest memories are of our grandmother, who had a warm and affectionate manner.

My youngest brother, Martin, the best cook in our family, is the owner of his own business, a beverage store. Like Burt and Susanne, he considers his biggest accomplishment to be his family—his wife Jodi and two children, Abby and Charlie. His thoughts of our upbringing turn to our father and his work ethic. He fondly recalls my grandparents catching small fish from the ocean and eating them right on the beach, raw and whole— another Italian delicacy.

I lived my first ten years in a three-bedroom house in Astoria, Queens. We lived with my grandparents, Massimiliano and Angela Tassielli, who were two of the most influential people in my life. As was Italian tradition, I was named after my grandfather, so Maximillian Michael Stangarone was my given name.

Ten of us in lived in a small house. And there were eight of us living in one bedroom on the top floor. There were two double beds, which slept four of us, and also a fold-out couch where my parents slept. Next to that was a youth bed. Needless to say, there was no privacy for any of us. After my little brother came along, five years after my twin sisters in 1968, I was bumped out of the upper floor and then slept on the middle floor with my grandparents. This was good timing because my Aunt Grace moved out at the time.

My grandparents truly were a second set of parents to me and my siblings.

My grandfather emigrated to America because times in Italy in the 1930s and 40s were extremely difficult and poverty-ridden. My grandparents and their five children lived in the poorest of conditions, with little hope for any future there. Three of my mother's siblings passed away in Italy due to illnesses. My mother had typhoid fever but survived.

So, my grandfather, Massimiliano, concealed himself in a ship in the spring of 1940 in the hope that America would be a better land, one that would fulfill his hopes and dreams for him and his family. He spent several days at sea in confined quarters but eventually he arrived safely in America. Sometime after he arrived, President Franklin Delano Roosevelt announced that if illegal citizens joined the armed forces they would be granted citizenship. So, he became a private in the United States Army (private first class, he would later proudly tell us) and served during World War II. It would be six years before he could send for his wife and his daughter Mary, my mother, and his son, Francesco, whom he hadn't even met since the boy was born after he left. Our family was from Sannicandro di Bari, a small village just on the Adriatic Coast in Southeastern Italy.

My grandfather lived with his brother in New Jersey when he first came over and worked various jobs. Then an opportunity came up in New York City to buy an ice and kerosene business, which he had for several years. Those were the days before refrigeration. Upon retirement, he became a doorman in an upscale apartment building in Manhattan. He always spoke of a woman who had a dog named Marmaduke, who was treated royally, better than some human beings.

My father, Vito Rocco Stangarone, was an extremely hard worker. He had several jobs and supported his large family, eventually owning a pizza place where he worked long hours. We wouldn't see him during the week—he would come home after bedtime and leave after we were off to school. I fondly remember the pizza he would leave in the refrigerator and I relished the thought of starting my day with a cold slice of pizza. He worked six to seven days a week and the only time we got to know him was when he opened up an Italian restaurant in Yonkers, NY. My older brother Burt would work as a pizza man and my younger brother Martin and I worked as busboys as teenagers. My father sacrificed a lot for his family. That was the way it was back then. My mother had five children in succession and sacrificed for her family as well. Thank God my grandmother was there to help out! To this day my mother is the most selfless woman I know.

What I remember most about my childhood was my grandfather. As I was his namesake, he treated me like a son. He was a strong, no-nonsense man who truly appreciated his adopted country and all its blessings. He often proclaimed, "God Bless America!"

My grandfather was my best friend. He took me everywhere he went, to visit friends, neighbors, and family members. He taught me how to play card games, which we played often—outside under his grapevines in the warmer months. He built a concrete pool with my father in his backyard for our family and friends, and grew grapes and made wine. He spent a lot of time with me.

I had a good relationship with my grandmother too when I was ten years old. She loved and nurtured all of her grandchildren even after we moved out to Long Island. She, too, had a phrase like my grandfather did that remains with me as an adult. Whatever challenge, whatever task was ahead, she would say to approach it "bel a bel," which in Italian means "nice and easy."

I fondly recall her as a very loving and giving person. She had one of the more difficult lives of all of my relatives, as she had to bear the responsibility of caring for her children alone for six years while my grandfather was making his way in the United States. She lived in poverty in Italy, without support of any kind, and had to shoulder alone the passing of three of her children. Thankfully she lived a good life in America until she was afflicted with Alzheimer's in her seventies; she passed away in 1992 at the age of 83.

My grandfather passed away in 1990 at the age of 81. He, too, had lived his dream in this country and sadly, had to watch his beloved wife suffer to this illness. My family believes that her deterioration led to his passing. Sometimes a broken heart can end a life.

My Uncle Frank, a teacher, guidance counselor, and later a published author, also spent a lot of time with me during my childhood. We would often play catch with a softball. On one of my most memorable childhood occasions, he took me and some friends to a Yankee game for my 10th birthday. At the game I received a card signed by the Yankees, a birthday cake, and between innings the scoreboard flashed "Happy Birthday Maxie," which was what I was affectionately called then. It was quite a thrill and I still fondly recall it to this day. Uncle Frank is still a role model for me.

I also remember one Christmas where I received one toy, a "Lost in Space" robot, which I treasured. I didn't need much in the way of material things, then or now.

On my father's side of the family, my grandparents were Umberto and Costanza Stangarone and I didn't see them often. My grandfather made furniture but he passed away much too early at the age of 63. I got to spend time with my grandmother as a teenager, staying at her house on weekends while working at my father's restaurant. I remember studying Italian my freshman year in college, and she was always there to help me with my studies. She even wrote a letter to my professor, Mr. Barrette, telling him of my progress. Every time I got some phrase down she would praise me by saying, "Perfetto." I believe this is where my father got his excellent work ethic. She was very disciplined, as well as loving and caring.

When we had family gatherings, especially for Christmas and New Year's Eve, they were filled with a joy and happiness that has never been equaled to this day. Everyone from my uncles and aunts and cousins, to my brothers and sisters, all gathered together and celebrated.

The women did the cooking and the men started playing cards after dinner—and they all played into the early morning hours. Upon opening his favorite bottle of champagne, Moet, my Uncle Pete sang the song "Noel, Noel," changing the lyrics to "Moet, Moet," every time a cork was popped. Fun was had by all. We were very close back then, especially my siblings and our cousins. We still see them a lot today. The bonding during those times was immeasurable. There were at least thirty of us during these functions.

As I look back at all the happiness, love, and joy in my childhood I can see now that this togetherness sustained me in my adult life, when more difficult days would come. Sometimes it's the little achievements in life that build foundations for bigger things to come, whether they are big successes or adversities that need to be overcome.

## Adolescence

My teen years were anything but joyful, unlike my childhood. I experienced a lot of anxiety and held low self-esteem. Looking back at my adolescence, I was probably experiencing mild depression and could have benefitted from medication and therapy.

Our upbringing in the 1970s was pretty rigid and my father insisted on quiet during the little time he was at home. Moods and feelings weren't openly discussed. Today however, children and adults more readily seek help for mood disorders.

Still, I carried on and saw that my perseverance in my adolescence from diligence with my studies to extra-curricular activities, to working at my father's restaurant, all contributed to the building of my character and my inner fortitude. My faith, firmly instilled in me during my childhood, greatly helped to prepare me for my biggest challenge to come: my battle with bipolar depression.

There were several things that helped me during difficult years of junior high and high school. Firstly, I loved to learn—I especially enjoyed math and science, and excelled in them. After school, I fastidiously did my homework and I felt a sense of accomplishment in my studies.

I also participated in extracurricular activities—I was in the chess club and ran track for two years, specializing in the 440-yard distance. I was a decent athlete. For one year, I ran on the cross-country team, which was the toughest endeavor I had ever undertaken. My coach was Mr. Gatto and he would have us practice twice a day, before school and after school. We would run several miles a day. It was good discipline for me and the meets were memorable. Our home field was Sunken Meadow State Park, which had the reputation of being one of the toughest courses in the state. There was one hill called "cardiac hill," which was incredibly steep and especially hard to traverse because it was covered with sand. I could feel my heart pump so loudly as well as a burning sensation in my lungs as I made my way to the top. By the end of the three-mile race I was quite exhausted but felt accomplished and exhilarated.

My elementary education began at Most Precious Blood, a Catholic school that was quite rigid. The school suited me and I was proud of my academic accomplishments. Going to a public school after Catholic school was a little like going to a zoo. Children disrespected the teachers, as opposed to Catholic school where any bad behavior would mean a crack across the knuckles with a ruler. One of the strictest teachers was Mrs. Cunningham, my third-grade teacher.

Throughout my teen years I was socially awkward with girls. Having braces and acne didn't help the matter. I had several guy friends but no female friends. I bonded with my brothers during this time and we formed a band, playing in the basement of our house. My older brother Burt played guitar, my younger brother Martin played the drums, and I played the bass guitar. We mostly played rock and roll, which we were raised on. I would go on to play in a band in college, which brought me great joy.

At the age of 15 I went to the movies with friends and saw what would be the most inspiring movie for me to date,—and still is to this day. That movie was "Rocky." Nothing before or since has ever spoken to me and resonated with me as much. The message of the triumph of the human spirit is what stayed with me. Later in life when I had manic episodes, I would often think of this movie. It somewhat kept me rooted in reality as part of my mind would enter into a psychosis.

My college years were filled with excitement and possibilities. For the first time, I had female relationships. I also had many other male friends as well, and it was truly the happiest time of my young adult life. I went to the State University of New York at Albany along with some of my friends from high school.

While tending to my studies, I also had a great social life. There were many parties and my outlook on life changed for the better. I was happy.

My friend, Charlie Perilla, and I formed a rock band where we played at parties and on one occasion played at the campus bar, the Rathskeller Pub for three nights (and actually got paid for it). To this day, I joke that I was a professional musician.

I became a member of Big Brothers and Sisters and served as a big brother to a boy named Rich during my sophomore year of college. Rich shared his unhappy childhood with me. His father had abandoned both him and his mother, who was struggling with her own issues and was just getting by. I took him to campus on a weekly basis and exposed him to the college life. He went to numerous activities with me, including games of the co-ed softball team that I managed. I hope I made some difference in his life.

Anyway, they were the best of times up until April of my senior year came and my illness came to take me from the joys of college to a future that was uncertain.

"The thought that we are enduring the unendurable is one of the things that keeps me going."
—Molly Haskell

# CHAPTER 2

## Be Your Own Advocate

When things seem hopeless and dark, and you feel isolated and alone, there is a tendency to stay on this never-ending treadmill but sometimes, though it may be brief, there is a light that comes through to us. It is then that we must do something—we must act—we must take that first step out of the seemingly endless darkness and reach out. My first inclination was to family. From there to medical doctors. Yours may be to a friend, a priest, a rabbi, a minister, or a medical doctor or therapist. This first step is the hardest but it must be done.

The fourteen years of the depressive phase of my illness were filled with trials—trials of dozens of medications and trials of multiple doctors. There were many setbacks and, in a word, it was disheartening. But I kept going. Call it sheer will or determination, but I knew that I was going to succeed in regaining restoration of my health.

So how do you get from your first diagnosis to a lifetime of wellness? You've just been diagnosed with bipolar disorder or major depressive disorder. There's nothing to be ashamed of. It's not an emotional fault within you. There isn't anything you've done to bring this on and it is generally quite scary. It is simply a chemical imbalance in the brain and it's treatable—period. Some are lucky and find the right treatment on their first try. Some, like myself, have to go through unrelenting levels of suffering for many years before they find what works for them.

## Don't Listen to the Naysayers

There are people out there who will tell you that your illness will keep you from functioning at your best, that it will keep you from leading a normal life. They will tell you that you will not improve. Some, like a couple of doctors I encountered, will tell you that you will improve somewhat but not all the way. Many will tell you to "accept" what God has given you and that there is nothing you can do about it. Don't listen to them. God's intentions for us is to be healthy and happy. Our responsibility is to find a way. While there are some illnesses in life that are irreversible, I also believe in miracles and cures, and I believe in the case of bipolar disorder or depression that you can not only get back to your old self, but that you can become even stronger because of the hardships that you encountered.

After my ECT treatments I was told by doctors to be satisfied for partial recovery and this was the best I could hope for. I must tell you this type of thinking made me very angry along the way. To eliminate this anger, as it did not serve me well in the long run, I told myself to continue to focus on the beliefs and goals I set for myself. This, for me, is still a work in progress, but I do my best to eliminate negative factors in my life. This is a constant and daily struggle of mine, but I believe that with time and patience, I will be able to disregard those who try to place limitations on me.

I believe anything is possible if you're willing to take the necessary steps—to seek out any and all help you can in the treatment of your illness. Keep a mindset of "I can" and "I will" and don't give up until you beat this illness. Listen to yourself—keep hope alive—persevere to that better day, no matter how long it takes. The world is full of people who believe in limitations, for themselves and for others. If I had listened to them I wouldn't be where I am today.

Remember that modern science is coming up with new medications, new treatments, all the time. Find a physician who is up to date on all the latest treatments.

I don't believe God's intention is for us to suffer all of our lives. Stick two thoughts in your mind, "I can" and "I will," and take the necessary steps toward your wellness. Never give up!

I have Bipolar disorder. Bipolar disorder causes distinct and uncontrollable changes in mood with simultaneous disturbances in energy, sleep, impulse control, concentration and activity level. The mood symptoms of bipolar disorder can also be understood as "mood episodes" that spread across a spectrum with varying combinations or grades of intensity.

The less severe form of mania is called a hypomanic episode. During a hypomanic episode, an individual can experience the same but less intense symptoms of a manic episode. The person may feel very good, be highly productive but exhibit uncharacteristic levels of energy or irritability coupled with changes in sleep, speech, self-esteem, concentration, thought and impulsivity. The symptoms may only be noticeable to family and friends. The symptoms are not severe enough to cause significant disturbance in function or change in daily activities or warrant psychiatric attention or hospitalization. However, there is the risk that a hypomanic episode could develop into a full manic or depressive episode without psychiatric treatment. It can also resolve on its own.

On the other end of the spectrum, a person with bipolar disorder can experience a depressive episode. This episode is indistinguishable from that seen in major depressive disorder. As per the DSM V, a person can feel depressed, sad and empty, or lose interest and pleasure, every day, in all or almost all activities for a consistent 2-week period of time. This mood disturbance is associated with decreased energy, fatigue, disturbances in sleep and appetite, diminished ability to think or concentrate, hopelessness, excessive guilt and low self-esteem. In its most severe point, a person can experience recurrent thought of death. The mood episode is severe enough to cause significant disturbance in function or change in daily activities or warrant psychiatric attention or hospitalization.

Frequently, bipolar disorder can invoke myriad symptoms of mania, hypomania and depression. This is called a mixed episode. During this episode, an individual can report feelings of depression, sadness and anger while outwardly appearing normal or happy, can have excessive amounts of energy, does not require much sleep and remains productive. The mood episode can be severe enough to cause significant disturbance in function or change in daily activities or warrant psychiatric attention or hospitalization.

It is important to exclude that the episodes are not caused by an underlying medical condition or a substance of abuse. An individual is diagnosed with bipolar disorder once he or she has a manic or hypomanic episode. Bipolar disorder, type 1, is defined by having at least one manic episode (with or without a depressive episode) and bipolar disorder, type 2, is defined by having at least one hypomanic episode (with or without a depressive episode).

Often, acute mania or depression, in the most severe stage,

can be complicated by psychosis. During this time, an individual can experience a disturbance in his or her understanding and perception of reality. A person can report delusions, defined as fixed, false, bizarre or illogical beliefs and/or hallucinations, which are sensory perceptions (auditory, visual, and olfactory) of something not actually present. Usually the psychotic episode resolves with the treatment associated with the acute manic or depressive episode.

## Best Health Organizations

Proper treatment is helpful even with those who have the most severe forms of the illness. One can gain better control of their mood swings and related symptoms. But because it is a lifelong illness, long-term continuous treatment is needed to control symptoms. With a licensed healthcare professional, define exactly what your mental disorder is, and seek out resources to become informed about what can help. Four national organizations have helped me a great deal. They are The National Institute of Mental Health, The National Alliance of the Mentally Ill, The Mayo Clinic, and the Depression and Bipolar Support Alliance. Their contact information is at the back of the book. They have a wealth of information, are eager to help, and are up to date on the latest scientific advancements for the treatment of the mentally ill.

## Seeking out Professional Help

I knew that even with the support of my family I had to seek out doctors and treatments on my own—and learned this early on in my illness. I went to about a dozen psychiatrists and several therapists in total during my illness.

If you do not have a supportive family, there are alternative avenues you can pursue for support. You can see a social worker, go to a mental health counselor, go to community mental health centers, a hospital psychiatric department, or an outpatient clinic. There are also mental health programs at universities and medical schools. Find family services, social agencies, or a priest or rabbi if you feel more comfortable. The Depression and Bipolar support alliance (DBSA) has peer or support groups in your area that you can join. Again, their contact information is in the back of the book.

The bottom line is to start somewhere, anywhere. You're not alone in this fight. And don't give up if one avenue you pursue isn't satisfactory. I ran into more than my share of dead ends with complacent healthcare professionals.

Most of the doctors I saw were on Long Island, where I lived, but I did go to Manhattan on a few occasions to see specialists in the field; one was an author of one of the numerous books I read on the subject, though he was of little help. Another, Dr. Sarah Lisanby, was the most knowledgeable and comprehensive doctor I worked with. She was at the time head of the Brain Stimulation Center at the New York State Psychiatric Institute. She examined every medication I had taken, noting that my lithium level was lower than the therapeutic dose. More importantly, she informed me that I had to stop taking this medication because it was doing irreparable damage to my kidneys.

She was at the cutting edge of research in this field and at the time was doing research studies on the treatment called "Transcranial Magnetic Stimulation," which is now widely used for the treatment of depression. While she did not give me a solution to my depression at the time, she did give me one huge intangible—hope.

She was the one doctor who assured me that there were new medications and treatments coming out all the time and it would only be a matter of time before my resolution was reached. She now is a psychiatrist at Duke University.

Many of the doctors I saw were content in not having me worsen rather than having my health restored. Others simply lacked compassion and showed little interest in my full recovery. At times I was disheartened, and, at times, furious at the lack of professionalism. One doctor told me that I should be glad I came this far after my ECT treatments and this was the best I could hope for. Settling for partial recovery just wasn't acceptable to me.

I was hospitalized several times due to my manic episodes, and on one occasion especially I was very distressed. My family put in a few urgent calls but my doctor at the time did not respond until the following day. She said that she had been hosting a party at her home and couldn't get back to them. I did not see her after that.

There are those doctors, like any profession, who simply go through the motions of work without caring or compassion for their patients. Thankfully, I found this type of physician to be few in number. Again, when I did come across one who was less than compassionate, I quickly changed to another doctor. Thank goodness for the ones who really cared. Without them, I don't know where I would be today.

There was one doctor who literally saved me twice. After my four and a half years of severe depression, having not responded to any medications, it was Dr. Marianne Hendrix who recommended that I try ECT treatments. This pulled me out of my deepest depression. Then after years of trials of medications, which took me into manic episodes and then back to moderate depression, I went to see her again—nine years later—in the hope that there was something I hadn't tried. She prescribed a newer medication, not an anti-depressant, but a mood stabilizer called "Abilify," which turned out to be the medication that pulled me all the way out of my depression and got me to wellness. Truly, thank God for Dr. Hendrix.

So if your doctor is simply prescribing you pill after pill, and has a complacent attitude of being satisfied with just some success, fight for your health. Don't stop seeking out doctors until you find one who truly cares about your *full recovery* and is up to date on the newest medications and treatments available.

Find the doctor who is willing to go that extra mile for you, one who recognizes and understands your unique situation, and helps you toward full recovery.

And this goes for therapists as well. Don't settle for the therapist that isn't committed to you, but find one, as I did, who is professional, competent, caring, and is willing to work with your psychiatrist. Again, someone who is willing to go that extra mile for you.

I believe I inherited bipolar disorder from my father's side of the family. This is the genetic side. There is also an environmental component to mental illness. Stressors, such as the loss of a job or a loved one, or any other negative experiences in your life, can trigger a manic or depressive episode. When I lost my job at Saint Claire's Hospital, a normal routine that was vital to my wellness was suddenly taken away from me.

When I first set out to write an article on my illness (initially I simply wanted to write a short article), I experienced hypomania. I felt good, highly productive, and a unique harmony in myself as the words flowed across the pages. I was up early in the morning for a couple of days. I got 6 hours of sleep instead of my usual 8. But while I was feeling good, due to previous experiences, an alarm went off in my head. Was I becoming manic? For me, the first thing I did was immediately get back to my normal eight hours of sleep. Sleep, medication, and relaxation techniques got me back on track.

My hypomania was a sign that if it was not addressed quickly it could become a full-blown mania. Thus, a manic episode was averted and I resumed normal functioning after a couple of days of good sleep.

## Support Groups

I admit in my journey through this illness that I did not reach out to others going through the same pain and suffering, other than through books. In retrospect, I realize that for many people support groups can be extremely helpful. Here are some reasons for joining a support group, which I derived from The Depression and Bipolar Support Alliance (DBSA). They hold local support groups throughout the nation. Their contact information is listed in the back of the book.

Support groups give you the opportunity to reach out to others and benefit from the experience of those who have "been there." They can help motivate you to follow your wellness plan, and they can help you understand that a mood disorder does not define who you are, and they provide a forum for mutual acceptance, understanding, and self-discovery.

Again, while you may find support groups a useful resource, they should complement qualified health and mental professionals that you work with.

## Setbacks

After seven years of stability from the "hellish" fourteen-year depressive aspect of these symptoms, I can tell you that I have had several setbacks in the manic part of this illness. The one big trigger for me is lack of sleep. This I must avoid more than anything else. I need eight hours of sleep. I can get by with seven, but nothing less than that. Proper sleep is important for me.

Again, it is imperative that you go over every medication you're taking with your doctor. It's best not to experiment on one's own, as only a licensed psychiatrist knows the interactions and side effects that occur when taking more than one medication. This is one area that there is no gray about it. Here I am very disciplined—I always go over medication adjustments with my doctor.

One of my strongest weapons against a manic relapse, which keeps me stable, is a steady work routine. I am fortunate to have full-time work during the week, which keeps me well grounded. I recently began working in a psychiatric hospital and one of my duties is to pick up charts from the various psych units. When interviewed at the start of this position the human resources director asked me if I had any reservations going to these units. Little did she know that I spent many manic episodes in the psych unit of a hospital, as well as an outpatient during my ECT treatments. I simply smiled at her and told her that I had no problem with this aspect of the job. I thought to myself, if she only knew of my past difficulties. I also believe that people inside psychiatric units of a hospital aren't crazy—in fact, many are more sane than those on the outside.

I still work for my brother on a part-time basis at the beverage store. The years I spent there probably saved my life. Having a place to go during difficult times, having interactions with people, and the physical nature of the job helped strengthen me and prevented me from having a relapse. It was the hardest time of my life. I dreaded going in most days, as part of me just wanted to stay at home. But the better part of me said, "Keep going, just keep going." And while it took years before my ship was righted the cumulative efforts molded me into more than just a survivor. I thrived at the end. I am positive that I would not be here today telling my story had I given up anywhere along the way. I feel it is at these critical times in one's life that it takes everything in your power to move forward—even an inch.

To my brother, Martin, I am truly grateful. For every time I had a setback, he welcomed me back to the store and this rising up every time I was knocked down I believe contributed to my overall health, more than medication itself, although I could not have succeeded without the combination of will and modern science.

What I want you to take away from my experience is that you come up with your own "game plan" on how to achieve wellness from either bipolar disorder or depression. A quote from Vince Lombardi comes to mind as I am writing this, "Keep going and you'll win." This applies not only in beating your illness but in future hurdles you will meet and clear thereafter!

## Family Support and Caregiving

Throughout my fourteen-year struggle to overcome the depressive phase of this illness, my family pitched in to help. My brother Burt gave me my first book to read entitled, *Win the Battle*, which inspired me and gave me hope. My sister Angela and my mother went to a conference given by NARSAD, a mental health research organization. Everyone took me to the doctor when I couldn't drive, including my sister-in-law, Jodi, and my brother-in-law Robert, and they never failed me. I remember staying at my brother Martin's house for several days during a manic episode because I couldn't be alone with this illness. I remember my twin sisters making me mac and cheese and grilled cheese sandwiches as comfort food.

I remember all of the support they gave me through all of my trials. I'm most grateful for my family for just being there, not judging me or telling me what was wrong with me, but all coming together for the little things, eating meals together, words of encouragement; there was very little conversation about accepting limitations. I am truly blessed in this regard. Thank God for my family, then and now.

If you know someone who has a mental illness, it may have an effect on you as well. The first and most important thing you can do is to help them get the right diagnosis and treatment. Encourage them to stay in treatment.

To help someone you care for, offer emotional support, understanding, patience, and encouragement. Learn about the particular mental illness so you can understand what your friend or relative is experiencing. Be a constant reminder that with time and treatment they can get better. Remind them that they are not alone, that others in their shoes have gone before them and successfully came out of it on the other side. An imperative: never ignore their discussions with you on the matter of harming themselves. *Always* report any such discussions to their healthcare professional.

How can caregivers find the support they need? Like many mental illnesses, dealing with someone who has bipolar disorder can be extremely difficult for family members, friends, and other caregivers. Relatives and friends often have to cope with serious behavioral problems, such as psychosis during a manic episode and withdrawal from society during depression.

The role of the caregiver isn't easy and it can take its toll. Their own stress may disrupt their life, cause physical and mental exhaustion, and strain relationships with those who aren't involved. It can be very difficult to cope with a loved one's behaviors due to their illness. According to the National Institute of Mental Health, one study shows that if a caregiver is under a lot of stress, his or her loved one has more trouble following the treatment plan, which increases the chance of a major bipolar episode. Therefore, you must take the time to take care of yourself.

From my own experiences, if you're a family member or friend of a loved one with a mental illness, support is the best advice I can give—caring, loving support.

No one wants to be depressed. No one asks for it. But sometimes God gives us hard and difficult experiences in order for us to grow, to be better and stronger individuals. As it's been said, "Don't pray for an easy life. Pray to be a strong person."

## Suicide

*Suicide is tragic. But it is also preventable.*

In being my own advocate I've relied on dozens of books by people who came through their own difficulty, survived it, and then thrived on the other side. This brings me to a topic that must be discussed. For whatever reason God spared me the thoughts and contemplations of suicide. It never entered my mind once through all of my suffering. But sadly, not everyone goes through difficulties and hopelessness without the thought of taking their own life.

Authors William Styron and Bob Olson thought of taking their own lives due to depression, the former planning out his demise with carbon monoxide poisoning, and the latter putting a gun to his head on more than one occasion. Fortunately, neither went through with it. Instead they wrote of getting through the hopeless periods of their lives and then gave hope to other people by sharing their stories.

Don't become a statistic. There is light at the end of the tunnel and the lives you touch after your ordeal may save countless lives. You're not alone in this. There are many people out there who will help you in any way they can.

It is also imperative to seek out a mental healthcare professional to talk to. Psychotherapy or "talk therapy" can effectively reduce and eliminate suicide risk. A psychiatrist can also administer medications that can alleviate your symptoms.

If you are reading this for someone who is in a crisis, don't leave him or her alone. If it is a true emergency get him or her to the nearest emergency room of a hospital, or call 911.

## Education

Through a licensed healthcare professional, define exactly what your mental disorder is, and then seek resources out that can help you.

Educate and seek inspiration to carry on to the next day. Along with literature I obtained from the major national mental health organizations, listed at the back of the book, I often went to the local bookstore to seek out the self-help and psychology sections for books on people overcoming their adversities. They inspired me and kept me going. So, keep reading and keep seeking. If you persist, you eventually will come out the other side of your illness—one filled with peace, hope, happiness, and a sound mind.

## You are not alone

Remember, you're not the only one out there with this illness. There are many who have gone before you and have prevailed. There are countless people, even many celebrities, who have been diagnosed with either having a major depressive episode or bipolar disorder in their lives and they are managing their disorders.

Don't give up hope, and when hope is dimmed, resolve to get through another day and look to a brighter day

I know it's hard firsthand, sometimes things seem insurmountable and even feel impossible, but make a firm resolve to seek out any help you can. The biggest lesson I've learned in my recovery is to take it one action, one day at a time.

These are two short lists of famous people, taken from Wikipedia, who have been diagnosed with a major depressive episode in their lives and who have been diagnosed with bipolar disorder.

First, those diagnosed with major depressive episodes:

> John Adams, second president of the United States
> Abraham Lincoln, sixteenth president of the United States
> Calvin Coolidge, thirtieth president of the United States
> Woody Allen, film director
> Halle Berry, actress

John Bon Jovi, singer/songwriter
Terry Bradshaw, professional football player, to analyst
Drew Carey, comedian
Ray Charles, singer
Johnny Carson, TV talk show host
Eric Clapton, singer/song writer
Courtney Cox, actress
Sheryl Crow, singer/songwriter
Rodney Dangerfield, comedian/actor
Ellen DeGeneres, comedian/talk show host
Emily Dickinson, poet
Bob Dylan, singer/songwriter
Harrison Ford, actor
Zack Greene, professional baseball player
Ken Griffey, Jr., professional baseball player
Jerry West, professional basketball player
Janet Jackson, singer
William James, American psychologist/philosopher
Billy Joel, musician
Alicia Keys, singer/songwriter
John Lennon, singer, songwriter
David Letterman, comedian/tv talk show host
Michelangelo, sculptor/painter
Conan O'Brien, comedian/talk show host
Gwyneth Paltrow, actress
Bruce Springsteen, musician/songwriter/singer
William Styron, writer
Mark Twain, writer
Mike Wallace, journalist
Walt Whitman, poet
Oprah Winfrey, TV talk show host/actress
Reese Witherspoon, actress

Second, the following famous people diagnosed with bipolar disorder:

> Catherine Zeta-Jones, actress
> Patty Duke, actress, author
> Dick Cavett, journalist
> Ludwig Van Beethoven, composer
> Charles Dickens, author
> Richard Dreyfus, actor
> Carrie Fisher, actress
> Mel Gibson, actor, director
> Ernest Hemingway, writer
> Jesse Jackson, Jr., politician
> Burgess Meredith, actor
> Kay Redfield Jamison, author of *An Unquiet Mind*, psychiatrist at Johns Hopkins University
> Margot Kidder, actress
> Cheri Oteri, actress, Saturday Night Live
> Jane Pauley, journalist, author
> Sidney Sheldon, author
> Charlie Pride, Country music artist
> Jaco Pastorius, jazz musician
> Brian Wilson, musician (Beach Boys)
> Virginia Woolf, writer

Believe you will win in your battle with mental illness. Many who have gone before you have succeeded.

"If we could give every individual
the right amount of nourishment and exercise,
not too little and not too much,
we would have found the safest way to health."
—Hippocrates

# CHAPTER 3

## Exercise Alters Brain Chemistry

Sometime during the ECT treatments and before I began working with my brother I knew that it was time to get up and move. Being sedentary physically was not going to improve my chances of getting well. Being moderately and less severely depressed led me to start exercising. My reason was twofold: 1) Mentally, I didn't want to go back to where I was before the ECT treatments and 2) Due to the medications I had been taking I gained over fifty pounds and physically wanted to get back down to my desired goal, 185. I had topped out on the scale at a weight of 242 pounds.

## Getting In Motion

I tell myself almost daily that an object in motion tends to stay in motion.

Before starting any exercise regimen, talk to your general doctor, or psychiatrist/psychologist/counselor, for guidance and support. Discuss an exercise program or physical activity routine and how it fits into your overall treatment plan.

Think realistically about what you are able to do and begin gradually. Tailor your plan to your own needs and abilities rather than trying to meet unrealistic guidelines.

Don't think of physical activity as a chore. Rather than a "should," view exercise as simply another tool to help you get better, like psychotherapy or medication.

Analyze your barriers. What's stopping you—break it down. For me, and for most, it is the initial step that's the most challenging.

Prepare for setbacks and obstacles. Give yourself credit for every step in the right direction, no matter how small. Keep at it, all the while recording it in a journal.

## Walking

Beginning any exercise program is not easy, especially after being sedentary for so long and still not feeling mentally well.

But I decided to make an effort to begin. There's a Christmas show that comes on every year called "Santa Claus is Coming to Town." In it, there is a depressed warlock whom Kris Kringle sings a song to. It is called "Put One Foot in Front of the Other." It simply states that putting one foot in front of the other will get you up and walking; at first simply across the floor, then eventually out the door. So, I did. One foot, one step at a time.

I started slowly and there were several stops and starts, but I persisted. I also started eating more moderately. I knew drinking eight glasses of water a day was recommended but I took it a step further. Before meals I would drink a lot of water to fill myself up and this helped a lot in reducing my food intake. I estimated that I drank well over a gallon of water a day during the year and a half it took me to lose the fifty pounds.

So anyway, I decided to get my sedentary body moving with the notion of shedding those fifty pounds and to hopefully help me with my mood.

I began by simply telling myself to get up and out the door, to get some fresh air, and to walk a few steps with no other goal in mind. It may seem like an easy thing to do, but when sedentary and depressed for quite some time this requires a great deal of effort. But looking back, it was worth it. It's been said that a journey of a thousand miles begins with one single step.

I then started walking up and down the block in my neighborhood. I started walking slowly and with little goals in mind like walking to the end of the street, then around the block, and so on.

After a while, I began to walk regularly. My goal was to walk every other day for twenty minutes, with a purposeful stride. Some weeks I attained this, some weeks I didn't, but I persisted and, most importantly, I wrote it all down. I logged every time I exercised and what I accomplished in my journal. Actually, seeing the progress on paper helped me immensely. And every Monday was my weigh-in day. At 242 pounds, getting to 185 was hard, but I gave myself short-term goals, five to ten pounds at a time. These little victories added up and I still remember to this day stepping on that scale and breaking the 200-pound barrier! This was a major milestone for me. Once reached, losing the remaining 15 pounds I needed came without quite the effort it took to lose the first 40 pounds. I admit that my weight loss wasn't always smooth sailing but perseverance and persistence paid off.

Walking is powerful medicine. According to the American Heart Association, if you walk thirty minutes a day five days a week, or 150 minutes a week, there are many benefits. Go to their website AHA.org.

So where do you begin? Start with the basics. All you need is a comfortable pair of sneakers and a place to walk (your neighborhood, a park, on a treadmill). I like to walk at the beach. After your initial trials and when ready, make a goal for the upcoming week. Then write it down.

After mastering getting out the door and taking those initial steps, a good follow up goal is walking ten minutes a day five days a week. If you do more or less to achieve your goal, write it all down. If less, then adopt the attitude of, "Well, I'll get 'em next time!" When you're feeling more motivated, shoot for fifteen to twenty minutes a day five days a week.

Again, as the weeks go by, track your progress. And always reward yourself for the little victories. For on them you can build bigger ones.

Then when you're ready, an ultimate goal of thirty minutes a day five days a week is great. If you happen to be one of those people who are more ambitious than that, then go for it! There are no rules but keep a basic structure and all the while keep writing it down.

By the way, if you have a dog, that thirty minutes can be broken into two fifteen-minute walks, one in the morning, and one later on.

My personal favorite place to walk is at the beach. I find it peaceful, tranquil, and calming. Also, getting some vitamin D from the sun helps with mood as well.

Walking does make a difference!

## Strength Training

After I began a walking routine, the opportunity came up to work with my brother at his store. So along with the cardiovascular exercise, lifting cases upon cases of beer and 170-pound kegs gave me muscle tone. After a period I began going to the gym. There are a few choices one can make as far as what type of strength training one can perform. I will tell you that my crowning achievement strength-wise did not occur in a gym. It came at my brother's beverage store. When I first began working there I could barely lift a keg off the ground. After a few years I handled it quite easily, until one day when a customer came in to pick up a keg. He had a bad back and asked me if I could put it in his truck. I said sure but when I went outside I saw this was no ordinary pickup truck. Its bed was almost shoulder high and before I attempted it I told myself to go for it. I bent at the knees (a cardinal rule for lifting heavy weights), turned the 170-pound keg on its side and in one swift and steady motion raised the keg up to my shoulders and slowly lowered it on to the bed of the truck. To this day I'm not quite sure how I did it. I think a little bit of mind over matter. Thankfully no other customer has made the same request since!

Like walking, strength training also has its benefits— some similar, some different. While strength training will add definition to your muscles and give men and women alike more toned muscles, there is so much more to be gained. Both make you stronger and can get you into better shape. With strength training your muscles need time to recover, so it should be done on alternate days. Always take time to warm up and cool down after strength training.

Some benefits of strength training:

1.  Strength training protects bone health and muscle mass.
2.  Strength training makes you stronger and fitter. Strength training is also called resistance training because it involves strengthening and toning your muscles by contracting them against a resisting force.
3.  Your balance, flexibility, and coordination will improve, as will your posture.

4. You burn calories during strength training, and your body continues to burn calories after strength training, a process called "physiologic homework." More calories are used to make and maintain muscle than fat.

There are more benefits to exercise in general:

1. It boosts happy chemicals. Exercise releases endorphins which create feelings of happiness or euphoria.
2. Improves self-confidence. On a very basic level, physical fitness can boost self-esteem and a positive self-image.
3. Exercise can be a way to enjoy the great outdoors. A little fresh air, sunshine, and exercise can work wonders for happiness.
4. It prevents cognitive decline. As we get older our brains get a little hazy. Working out boosts the chemicals in the brain that support and prevent degeneration of the hippocampus, an important part of the brain for memory and learning.
5. It boosts brainpower. Cardiovascular exercise can create new brain cells (neurogenesis) and improve overall brain performance.
6. Increases relaxation. A moderate workout can be the equivalent of a sleeping pill for people with insomnia.
7. You will get more done. People who take time for exercise on a regular basis are more productive and have more energy than their sedentary peers.
8. You may inspire others. Even fitness beginners can inspire each other to push harder during a session, so join a club. There is a website called meetup.com, which has all types of group exercises, like walking, jogging, rock-climbing, and much more.

Exercise became a stabilizing force for me. Through all of my time at the beverage store I didn't revert to the deep depression. As I went through my ups and downs from manic to moderate depression, I never again sank into the severe depression that I experienced at the onset of my major depressive episode. It has now been several years and part of my mental health I owe to taking care of myself physically.

I will briefly mention that in losing the fifty pounds, hand in hand with exercising, I ate more moderately, and I chronicled this in a daily journal as well. I knew this was as important as exercising.

Medications, specifically, was the number one reason for my weight gain of over fifty pounds. The medications I was on, especially Zyprexa, makes you feel hungry. I remember going to the refrigerator at all hours of the night, getting anything I could find to eat just to satisfy my cravings.

When I finally had enough of my large belly, which I never had in my life up until this point, I decided to do things a bit radically. I gave myself a 1200 daily calorie intake. For a 240-pound male, this amount was less than sensible. Still, I tried it for a short period of time but found it very difficult to maintain. I stopped and started numerous times but again, the road to weight loss isn't one of starvation. I would lose ten pounds and then put it back on quickly.

I then bought the diet frozen food meals and tried that unsuccessfully as well. Again, its premise wasn't good from the start-again another way of starving one's self. So, after experimenting with these and a couple other fad diets, I finally came to the conclusion that gradual weight loss was the way to go. After reading up on several weight loss programs and noticing that the food portions were critical to weight loss, I felt moderation was the way to proceed. If they were fit and trim in Europe, then I could be as well.

The most sensible thing I did was to cut my portions by one third. Again, not so simple to keep, but I was determined and reached a goal in the mid-180s where I've basically stayed for the last few years. Again, it took me roughly over a year and a half to lose the fifty plus pounds, but after I did I never looked back. I also gave myself one day during the week to eat whatever I wanted—a reward for the healthy six days.

The beginning of any weight loss program is difficult because it is similar to beginning exercise in this respect. Also, it's good to know that newer medications are coming up all the time that have less of an effect on you in regard to weight gain.

I guess for me there's no other way to put it –willpower, persistence, and discipline. I lost roughly three pounds a month on average but I did it. As far as maintenance is concerned, now I give myself two days to eat what I want and have five days of healthy eating. A great weight loss program which many friends and family have undertaken successfully is Weight Watchers.

Many family members and friends have successfully lost weight on this diet. They stress eating more fruits and vegetables, allow you to eat what you want, in moderation of course, and reward you for any exercise you do.

In an article in *U.S. News and World Report*, they rank Weight Watchers as one of the top three diets. Their theory is that there is more to dieting than counting calories—if you make healthy choices that fill you up you'll eat less. Weight Watchers PointsPlus program assigns every food a point value, based on its protein, carbohydrate, fat, or fiber. Choices that fill you up, the longest "cost" the least, and nutritionally dense foods cost less than empty calories. So, if you're deciding between a two hundred calorie iced coffee and a hundred calorie smoothie, the smoothie is the better choice.

You can eat whatever you want provided you stick to your daily PointsPlus target, a number based on your gender, weight, height, and age. A big selling point for me is that you can load up on fruits and vegetables, as they carry zero points. Thus, you can eat as much as you like since they're high in fiber and more filling than, for example, a bag of chips, or a candy bar.

By promoting weight loss, the program can help with Type 2 diabetes. Losing just five to ten percent of your current weight can stave off many diseases, as is also the case with exercise.

Weight Watchers also offers emotional support and group meetings that can lead to a higher compliance than a diet practiced alone. What I especially like about this program is that no food is off limits. If you're craving cheeseburger, go for it. Weight Watchers simply helps you control portions and alter your favorite recipes so your meals are as healthy as possible.

Another great thing about Weight Watchers is that exercise is encouraged. They assign a PointsPlus value to a number of activities, such as walking, dancing, or cleaning, which are listed online. These count as extra food points, which allows you to splurge every so often. For example, if you do an activity three or four times a week you can "spend" your extra points on a second slice of pizza, or a meal at your favorite restaurant. Weight Watchers recommends using everyday activities to get more active. You get points for doing household chores such as doing laundry. You can go to their website, weightwatchers.com for more information.

Weight loss contributes to physical health but mental health is just as important. Choose an attitude of health. I woke up and still do with an attitude that I would persevere through the day and see myself to an ultimately brighter day. My mental health was a much more difficult battle than my physical one, but I also kept an attitude of hope and faith on a daily basis until I triumphed. Attitude is a key to success.

"Writing in a journal reminds you
of your goals and of your learning in life.
It offers a place where you can hold a deliberate,
thoughtful conversation with yourself."
—Robin S. Sharma

# CHAPTER 4

## Writing and Keeping a Journal

I don't know where I would be today if I didn't write. Writing for me was a form of release and one of great encouragement. You can write one word or several pages but make it a habit to write something daily. During my darkest days I could only manage a simple phrase like, "Hang in there," or "Where there's a will, there's a way." But I got a sense of accomplishment from this: simply writing something encouraging keeps you going for another day, until ultimately, you find that better day.

I write every morning when I get up and most evenings when I get home from work. It is healing in and of itself. In the book, "The right to write," Julia Cameron states that "writing is medicine, that it is an appropriate antidote to injury. It is an appropriate companion for any difficult change!"

When I feel that there is nothing in me to write, I start

with words and thoughts of gratitude – simply being thankful for my family, a roof over my head, food on the table, and now, thankfully, for my health. Also, I think of my doctors. Though I'd been to many there were a few who were most helpful and I write down their names with a special thank you. Dr. Marianne Hendrix, who initially recommended my ECT treatments when no medications worked, after seeing her several years later, she ultimately gave me a medication that finally led me to regain my health and reclaim my life again. Second, to Dr. Helen Baietto, my therapist who helped guide me to wellness in all aspects of my life. Lastly to Dr. Maria Benetos, a most intelligent and, more importantly, a most compassionate, truly one in a million doctor.

Throughout this chapter I will give a few excerpts from my journals over the last several years, from the depths of depression to more hopeful, better times.

Sometimes, with little hope it takes sheer will to continue on. Here are some of my journal excerpts:

> *During a steep portion of my depression:* "Our resolve now is to hope for a much better tomorrow. It does not feel good to feel like an inferior being over the past several years. We've certainly had enough. This is not what God wants for us. To describe feeling inferior, to fear any and all conversation with all other people, to dread it. This is not what God intended. We persevere to another day."

> *On a more thankful, hopeful day:* "We truly are lucky to be living in this country. Something that goes through our mind is our grandparents and parents and how hard their lives were before they came to this country. 'God Bless America!' as my grandfather would say on an almost daily basis."

*On modern science:* "We are having more breakthroughs each day toward cures for illness and diseases. We have come far in the treatment of bipolar illness and also will be coming out with newer and better treatments and medications all the time. One day there will be a cure for cancer, cures to mental illness, to paralysis, to all illnesses and diseases in life. It is for us to persevere until we reach a better day. Thank goodness we live in this country."

Another thankful, hopeful day.

Every thought, every small action helps our state of being.

Give good advice and encourage others always. Cherish all that we have, enjoy our days, stop and smell the roses, and, in more trying times endure without complaint. Always persevere. In good times and enduring times that we go forward with strength, enthusiasm, optimism, faith—in God and in ourselves, and hope that there will be a better day here on earth.

Jim Valvano said that his cancer would not defeat him. He never gave up. He lost his battle, but encouraged others and inspired others never to give up on life's challenges.

Finally, be thankful for the day, know that God hears us all, that we may proceed with a lighter heart and to impart this enthusiasm to others.

If we can make a positive difference to even one person in one lifetime, then we have achieved. To leave this world a better place for us having been in it, this is our aim.

I have been blessed in many ways, from my family, to a roof over my head, to food on the table, and a good, strong state of being.

We have a choice in our lives. To choose to be our best self, more compassionate, more kind, more loving and forgiving, to be bright and enthusiastic, to be less selfish and more selfless, to always think positive, to choose virtue over vice, to believe in ourselves.

To be thankful on a daily basis for our men and women who defend our country, they are the most courageous people on this earth…

As we go forward with a clear conscience, peace of mind and a resolve to be our best selves, a determination to see all things through until a resolution is reached, and a determination to be happy. Abraham Lincoln said, "Folks are about as happy as they make up their minds to be."

Writing, it has been proven, positively affects your mood. In a study by James Pennebaker, psychologist and author of the book *Opening Up*, he shows that expressive writing, or writing about traumatic issues in your life leads to mood change. He says that there is a therapeutic aspect to writing that leads not only to psychological changes but to biological and behavioral changes as well. According to his study, drops in blood pressure, heart rate, changes in brainwave patterns, increases in general immune system function have all been observed after writing about a trauma.

Also, as I had mentioned in a previous chapter on exercise, journaling helped me to track my exercise and diet as I needed to lose in excess of fifty pounds due to some of the medications I was prescribed. Weight problems don't have to defeat you. Write down a plan, a goal, as I have shown in the chapter on exercise.

## Benefits of Journaling for Depression

Keeping a journal for depression can be a very positive and useful tool. Anne Lamott, in her book *Bird by Bird*, discusses writing without edits. She states that to effectively write, one should write whatever comes to mind the first thing in the morning and to fill up three pages with this—even if you write the same thing over and over again. And don't edit yourself. Just let your thoughts flow free. This is the beginning of expressive writing.

By writing routinely you will get to know what makes you feel happy and confident, and you will know yourself better. You feel clearer about situations and people who are toxic for you—important information for your emotional well-being. Writing about anger, sadness, and other painful moments helps to relieve the stress and intensity of these feelings. By doing so you will feel calmer and better able to stay in the present. Writing is an outlet for your feelings. Many times, you just need to let your thoughts, emotions, and feelings out. Although talking to a trusted friend, family member, or healthcare provider/therapist is the best way to achieve this, sometimes a journal for depression is a great alternative. Many times, we are not sure of why we are feeling down, hurt, or anxious, but writing things down forces us to find the underlying reasons.

Writing is a great way to problem solve. Writing down the underlying issues can be a great tool. When we journal for depression, we truly identify the issues that truly bother us, and are better able to solve that very problem. It's also a way to keep a log of your feelings. Sometimes during weekly counseling meetings one can forget what the issues have been for the week. I always go to my doctor with a prepared version of my past week to re-hash anything that might be of importance. Keeping a journal allows you to track patterns, trends, improvement and growth over time. When certain circumstances appear insurmountable, you will be able to look back on previous dilemmas that you have since resolved. Write as if you were writing to a trusted friend. In the end, I became my own best friend.

Begin with writing all of the things you are grateful for. This has the virtue of interrupting the self-centeredness that depression tends to provide. Writing things you are grateful for forces your mind to brainstorm to something positive, and makes the mind acknowledge that there are things still enjoyable in life. Record specific problems in your journal. If there is something that causes you anxiety or worry, write it down because it harnesses your brain to lock down on specifics, not to ruminate on vague thoughts.

Thank your journal for listening. A quick thank you note suffices. This accomplishes two things, self-respect and respect for what you have shared in your journal. Your thoughts and emotions are true and real, and your journal is a real outlet, and a friend that can always be there to receive all your feelings empathetically. This also gives you a feeling of closure with your journal and you can then continue with the rest of the day.

Journaling can be a very useful tool for your depression self-help. Journal when you want and need to. Journal daily when you can—again first thing in the morning is great, or whenever you have an urge to express your feelings.

Here are another couple of excerpts from my journals (This is from where I had to take a four-month break from the beverage store as my doctor experimented with medications without any success after the onset of a manic episode with moderate depression.):

> Yesterday was a most disheartening day. We are still unable to process information and our mind is still stuck. It has now been fourteen weeks. We don't know what to tell ourselves at this point. Will this illness ever leave us? Will it ever subside? Today, a little helplessness, a little distraught, a great deal of weighing on our heart as to what I can do now. The only positive that while not improving, and a big positive, we are not going backwards. Again, the inability to think, the most disheartening feeling of all. Just to hope and pray for continued improvement and stability.

More hopeful days:

> From where we are now all we want to focus on is
> our present and our future and to keep with us the
> notion of "Onward and Upward" as we persevere
> through our lifetime.

> Our fiftieth birthday is approaching this year and
> we just hope that 2011 is a good year.

> We firmly believe there is a heaven and have faith
> in God and in ourselves. We plan on helping
> people with this illness in some capacity. We have
> a sense within us of all that is right and good and
> these ideals will emanate from me. We adhere to
> the idea that what we do is an extension of who
> we are. We were certainly raised right, from our
> parents to our grandparents, and to others who
> have come into our lives. We still believe in true
> love and this is one of the more important things
> that keeps us going.

> We believe there are like-minded thinkers out
> there who urge us on, again those in this world
> and those that have passed.

> That we aspire to be our best selves, moral,
> idealistic. That we have a strong faith in God,
> that there is a Divine Guidance in all matters, not
> just in our vocation.

> Compassion to those who are less fortunate
> but not ever to give up on them, to believe in
> miracles—big and small. To hope and pray, to be

inspired and thus to inspire is our aim. To succeed in our endeavors with hope and thus give hope to others.

To think on life's simplicity—love of God, love of family, love between a man and woman or a significant other. To thank God, thank goodness for all we do have from our relentless pursuit of our mental health, for a roof over our head and an abundance of food on our table. Lastly, our family, who without their support, we could not have continued. In these respects, we are truly blessed.

Much of my writing is of a prayerful nature. I write through all days, whether they are great days or difficult days; through times of hope and inspiration and times when my hope is dimmed. This simple discipline keeps me moving forward.

I write for encouragement, inspiration, new ideas, the best course of action to follow each day and thankfulness. I pray that I put in my best effort each day. For myself I mostly write to further strengthen myself, for Trust and Confidence in God and for the same Trust and Confidence within myself.

"He who has faith has an inward reservoir
of courage, hope, confidence, calmness, and ensuring trust
that all will work out well,
even to the world it would not seem so."
—B.C. Forbes

# CHAPTER 5

## Faith, Determination, Perseverance, Hope, and Victory

Regardless of what adversity, obstacles, or opposition we may face, it is of the utmost importance that we persevere. If we adopt a "never give up" mentality, we will overcome all that is thrown our way. We will emerge from adversity a stronger and better person, more appreciative of things we lost during more difficult times.

### Determination

My grandfather taught me one thing. He came to this country with a dream, that he and his family would have a better life, and he fulfilled his dream with one thought in mind—Determination.

He instilled in his family this same resoluteness to see our dreams fulfilled. I thank him most for that.

## Faith

Faith....is a higher faculty than reason.
Faith...is a sounder guide than reason.
Faith....has no limits.

I have always had a simple faith in God—that He knows what's best for us—to do the best we can and to leave the rest to Him.

When I was at the young age of eight, I became an altar boy at Most Precious Blood Church in Astoria, Queens. Along with what I believe was being born with an innate faith, through Catholic school, church and a religious family, I always had an unshakeable faith in God.

Being an altar boy taught me discipline and respect for the priests and elders. Then on to adulthood where my faith would be put into practice.

On my journey through life and specifically battling and ultimately being victorious over this illness, I have developed a good deal of strength and feel more of a nearness to God and His plans for me.

For reasons unknown at the time, when my depression first manifested itself in February 1998 at the age of thirty-six, I got myself a legal pad and began writing daily.

Mostly, at the beginning of what would be a fourteen-year depression, were words of faith and encouragement. I would write, "Have faith in God. Have faith in ourselves." This simple statement is something I would write most often. Also, simple words of encouragement like, "Hang in there" and "Where there's a will, there's a way." As the first several months wore on with nothing but pain and darkness, I said to myself, "Some way, somehow, I am going to beat this illness."

Later as I continued to write (I also read books of inspiration and hope from people going through their own adversities), one thought was on my mind almost daily. This thought still remains with me today. Simply stated, "Don't give up; don't ever give up!", a quote from Jim Valvano, a great college basketball coach who showed unbelievable courage in his battle with cancer. On March 3, 1993, he gave an inspirational speech at the ESPY awards, one that touched me deeply. He was the recipient of the Arthur Ashe Courage Award. In his speech, he states that to have goals and dreams are a must in this life. And you have to work hard to make your dreams become a reality. He went on to quote Emerson. "Nothing great can be accomplished without enthusiasm."

He also stated that regardless of what problems life presented to you never give up. He battled his illness to the end but eventually lost his fight against cancer.

Jim Valvano did, however, start the "V" foundation for cancer research, and twenty years later his foundation has raised hundreds of millions of dollars for cancer research. He also said in that speech that this foundation may not save his life, but it may save the life of someone you love. He went on to say, cancer cannot touch my mind. It cannot touch my heart, and it cannot touch my soul, and these three things shall last forever. His spirit has touched many. After seeing his speech again and again, I was determined not to be beaten.

If I listened to reason I would not be here today. If I listened to those who threw statistics at me about why I would not fully recover, or find regular work I would not be here today. If I listened to the voices of many who said to simply 'accept' what God has given me I would not be here today. If I listened to all the naysayers who said 'you can't' I would not be here today writing my story.

You see, faith is a higher faculty than reason. I was given dozens of reasons as to why I would not fully recover but something within me told me differently. This something—faith—an innate belief in God and myself told me not to listen to anyone but myself. And my inner self told me 'yes', I would find a way out of this regardless of how long it would take. This is the only thing I listened to. I believe God wants us to be healthy and happy, though trials and suffering may be part of His plan. Helen Keller said that while the world is full of suffering it is also full of the overcoming of it. So, if your illness is depression or bipolar disorder, follow all resources you have and know that modern science is always coming up with newer and better treatments and medications and I know that one day, maybe not in my generation but in future generations there will be breakthroughs and ultimately cures.

I also kept written affirmations everywhere. I taped on my bathroom mirror a paper on which read, "Where there's a will, there's a way." And in my wallet I've kept, and still keep, this quote from Michelangelo, the genius painter and sculptor, which reads, "Faith in one's self is the best and safest course." Don't listen to the negative on the outside, but have faith in yourself, believe in yourself. You have the answers within you! A final thought on faith: Vince Lombardi says when we plan our dependence on God we are unencumbered, and we have no worry. This confidence, this sureness of action, is both contagious and an aid to the perfect action. The rest is in the hands of God.

## Hope and Inspiration

Sometimes in going through this type of illness, hope is quelled. But there are ways we can give ourselves some help in this respect. We can feed ourselves positive information, whether it stems from writing, or reaching out to outside sources such as family, friends, doctors, music, movies, and books can also be a source of hope and inspiration.

There's a song sung by Elvis Presley called, 'If I can dream,' which gave me hope and inspiration throughout my illness. It basically is about living in this world, which is a difficult world to be in, to have hope as you gain strength on your path in life. The song also says to dream for a better world for yourself and for humanity, that somewhere there is a heaven, and to have faith over fear.

Again, while the world isn't perfect one can dream and believe in a better outcome. In addition, for inspiration, I drew on many books, for reason to go on another day. The first book I read was given to me by my older brother Burt, the most generous person I know. The book was entitled, *'Win the Battle'* by Bob Olson. In it, he tells of his five-year battle with depression, his contemplation of suicide, but in the end he stuck it out and it was all worth it. I read this book over and over, at least a dozen times. I am fortunate for my make-up that I never let the thought of suicide enter my mind, and this was something that I'm sure came from somewhere up above.

As I learned, you must be your own advocate. Sometimes, I found myself alone, isolated, without much hope, but I said continuously to myself, "some way, somehow", and continued making appointments with doctors (I saw several) and reaching out to family, and was always writing. Writing is a powerful medicine in itself and I will explain its benefits in another chapter.

Be a story of triumph over adversity. You're not only saving your life, but your story can help save the life of another, it can offer them hope and inspiration for their fight.

Bob Olson ends his book with, "To have hope, to succeed with hope, to give hope to others." Choose hope, it's all worth it in the end. And when hope is dimmed, resolve to persevere to another day, a better day.

## Perseverance

Perseverance has come to be my favorite word in the English language. Its definition is continued effort to do or achieve something despite difficulties, failure, or opposition; the action or condition or an instance of persevering; steadfastness.

A quick story on perseverance: When my sister Connie was a student in high school, she wasn't that interested in her studies. If she received a C, she accepted it. Her expectations were low. After high school, she worked for a few years as a dental assistant before deciding on going to a community college. She switched schools and majors several times, studying varied subjects from nutrition to the arts. She stopped and started several times over several years, finally receiving her bachelor's degree from Stony Brook University at the age of 30. But she was not finished there. She went on to get her master's degree from Temple University in the field of social work. She now is a successful social worker in a school district in Brooklyn, NY. Had she not kept up with it anywhere along the way, she would not have the satisfaction of having her successful life. She did not give up.

All of my five brothers and sisters have found their own successes due to what I believe was the way we were raised. Our values of hard work were instilled in us from our parents, Italian immigrants who came to the United States with nothing but the ideals of hard work, sacrifice, determination, hope, faith and love.

## One's Attitude

There's one thing I've had during my illness which is the attitude of never giving up. While you can't choose what happens to you in your life, you can choose how you will react and feel and how you respond to it.

My niece Abby was diagnosed with Chiari malformation which is a condition in which headaches are caused due to pressure in the cerebellar part of the brain. She was only 12 years young at the time. Her condition required brain surgery. The bravery she showed leading up to, during, and after the surgery, was remarkable. She was calm in the days preceding the operation, and I remember her lying in the hospital immediately after the surgery knowing the pain she was in and she bravely endured it without complaint. She was given morphine at the time. She could have cried and complained but she didn't. She chose this way to deal with something most of us will never have to encounter in our lifetime. Hers was true courage. A few years later she is a member of the National Honor Society Music and Italian Honor Society, participates in cross-country running, was a Vice President of Student Council, and is an extremely talented and dedicated musician. There's something to be said about looking at one's life and problems relative to something children like Abby go through. She is a strong and determined young woman.

Norman Vincent Peale, author of *The Power of Positive Thinking*, also states that forces beyond your control can take everything you possess except one thing, your freedom to choose how to respond to that situation. You cannot control what happens to you in life, but you can always control what to do about what happens to you.

And on winning your battle with depression, I look to Vince Lombardi, a great football coach who also had a great philosophy on life. He said, "Winning isn't everything, it's the only thing." Commit in your mind that you're going to win your battle. There is much to learn from a winning attitude.

In my favorite series of movies, "Rocky," the main character states, "Life ain't all sunshine and rainbows. It can beat you to your knees. But if you can get up and keep moving forward, that's how winning is done."

These are just a few examples of people choosing to push through adversities thrown their way. I looked and sought out any books and movies I could of people victorious over their struggles.

During my time working at my brother's store I went from depression to mania several times, and with each setback I had to stop working at the store, sometimes for days, sometimes weeks, and on a couple of occasions, months. But, after every time I suffered a setback, I returned to the store. It doesn't matter how many times we fall, what matters is getting up and moving forward if you do have a setback.

## On Achieving Victory–With Your Illness and Beyond

My goal after achieving my health, was to write a book that would help others in persevering and to give them hope, hopefully inspiring them to continue on to the day when their suffering will end and their lives will begin anew. A few simple thoughts on how I've proceeded toward fulfilling my goals.

1) Self-trust is the first key to success. I've learned to take life one day at a time and I pray for a unity with and under God, and to stay the course toward my goals and dreams.
2) Have a clear goal or goals in mind. For myself, helping others with this book and being healthy in all aspects of my life-physically, mentally, spiritually, and socially.

I then looked to people who inspire me like Vince Lombardi, Jim Valvano, and Norman Vincent Peale on how to proceed to achieve this goal. In *The Essential Vince Lombardi* by Vince Lombardi, Jr., he states, "A person can be as great as he wants to be. If you believe in yourself and have the courage, the determination, the dedication and if you are willing to sacrifice the little things in life, and pay the price for the things that are worthwhile, it can be done.....That victory must be pursued, with every bit of our mind and all of our effort."

So, I started writing towards this end. I wasn't quite sure where it would lead me, but I started writing about my experiences, reading all of my old journals, going to the bookstore often, researching anything that came to mind. And then, from there, chapters formed and things fell into place.

Norman Vincent Peale had a strategy for goal setting, which I used during the writing of this book. To sum up, first organize all the elements of yourself so that they are harmonious toward and to your goals. Second, pray about your goal. If it's a worthy goal it will come about.

Next, visualize or picture your goal(s) clearly. It will sink into your subconscious mind.

Expect the best-think confidently. Last, visualize yourself achieving and having a sustained effort.

Unforeseen problems may arise toward attaining your goals and dreams but again they are to be pursued persistently.

I hope your goals will be set and met. Always remember smaller victories lead to bigger victories.

My first goal was achieving my health again. I took the necessary steps toward that goal. I went to all my doctor's appointments, took my medication religiously, and I wrote, read, and prayed daily. I started exercising, again with smaller goals at first like getting off the couch and walking a few steps, then walking out the door…until I found and sustained a regular exercise schedule.

Again, doing one's best and understanding that setbacks do occur, are part of the process to victory. The key is getting up after each setback and to continue to move forward.

To sum up, we can't control what happens to us in life, but how we respond makes all the difference in the world. Have faith in yourself. Where there's a will there's a way and where there is no way, God will find a way. And keep going. Sylvester Stallone says that what made him a successful man was not that he was the most talented individual in the world, but he kept going and going and going. Perseverance is your best ally to achieve your victory in your battle with mental illness and beyond, to future victories that lie ahead.

Every little thing you do from your attitude to reading to writing to watching inspiring movies all add up. Don't think that the little things we do don't matter. They all matter in your battle. So, give it all you've got. You'll come out on top.

To quote the great Vince Lombardi, "Keep going and you'll win."

"Hope is the feeling you have
that the feeling you have is not permanent."
—Jean Kerr

# CHAPTER 6

## My Experiences with Therapy

Psychotherapy is a valuable and crucial tool in the treatment of depression, bipolar disorder, and life's general problems as well.

"Psychotherapy or 'talk therapy' is a way to treat people with a mental disorder by helping them understand their illness. It teaches people strategies and gives them tools to deal with stress and unhealthy thoughts and behaviors. Psychotherapy helps manage symptoms better in order to function at their best in everyday life.

Sometimes psychotherapy alone is the best treatment for a person depending on the illness and its severity." For me, psychotherapy was most helpful in combination with medications.

There is still some stigma seeking help for emotional and health problems, including depression and bipolar disorder. Unfortunately, as was the case when I was first diagnosed, many view mental illness as a sign of weakness rather than as a signal that something is out of balance. And as is with the case with depression, people cannot simply snap out of it and feel better automatically.

Many people with mental illness who don't seek help suffer needlessly. Keeping emotions bottled up or keeping them to oneself accompanied by a sense of isolation can worsen the illness. If any mental illness goes untreated it can last for a long time and worsen over time.

Skilled health and mental healthcare professionals can work with individuals who have mental illness to:

1) Pinpoint the life problems that contribute to their illness, and help them understand which problems they may be able to solve or improve. A licensed professional can help patients identify options for the future and set realistic goals to improve their emotional well-being.
2) Identify negative or distorted thought patterns that contribute to feelings of hopelessness and helplessness that accompany illnesses like depression.
3) Develop skills that relieve suffering and prevent later setbacks of their illness. Some of these skills may include developing or strengthening social networks, creating new ways to cope with challenge, and making a personal self-care plan that includes positive lifestyle changes.

For many, medications, along with psychotherapy, are helpful for reducing symptoms of mental illness, specifically depression.

By conducting a thorough assessment, a licensed and trained mental health professional can help make recommendations about an effective course of treatment for each individual and his or her specific problems and needs.

## My First Experience with Psychotherapy

At the age of twenty-eight, after five years of stability from my initial manic episode, I was not very happy with my work situation. It served my purpose until this point in time. I was an accountant and a regular, steady job brought me stability. This was indeed very therapeutic for me. I socialized with work colleagues and other friends, took vacations and in general led a normal, balanced life. Something, though, was lacking—some type of meaning to what I was doing.

So, I decided to see a therapist. I went to see Dr. Flo Rosof who was highly recommended and see what I could do to improve my situation. One of the first things she did was to give me the first of many books to read under her tutelage. It was called *What Color Is Your Parachute?* by Richard Nelson Bolles, and, I began working on areas to explore for my next vocation. I was strong in the sciences back in high school and as was my nature, I liked to interact with people and help others in some capacity.

As we went about discussing areas of interest the health field seemed to be a good match for me. While I didn't know specifically what specific area to go towards she simply told me to pick one and from there I would be led into a more suitable area—simply at that point to trust my instincts—this a phrase she repeatedly drummed in me until it indeed became second nature to me.

So, I chose the profession of radiologic technology and it did give me a lot more satisfaction than accounting did. I saw Flo for roughly two years until I entered Long Island University and at the age of thirty-two obtained my second bachelor's degree.

Flo not only helped me with my occupational direction she also introduced me to many psychologically based books that enlightened me and gave me a structure on how to proceed in life in general. She was a very wise and gentle soul. She fed me books by humanists like Carl Rogers to existential thinkers Soren

Kierkegaard and Victor Frankl, the author of *Man's search for meaning*, which I read many times.

I would see her on a weekly basis and each week she would give me a card with a thought or phrase to think on for the week. Some of her wise notes were:

> Fear is not a stop sign.
> Go as slowly as possible. (Abraham Lincoln is quoted a number of times as saying to go slow and easy).
> Do the best you can, the results are not in your hands.
> You will be led.
> Trust your instincts.
> Keep moving forward.
> Feelings are not the whole story... Dr. Rosof helped me to mature.

She taught me the value of being appreciative of the things that I did have in my life at the moment, not to focus on what I did not have. She reminded me that people who had gone through the most difficult of circumstances were more appreciative than those who had not. She also reinforced in me that kindness and goodness were the most important traits one could have.

So, I didn't just have a career coach but I found a life coach as well. She laid the foundation for me to be stronger, better, and imparted some of her wisdom as well. To her I am very thankful.

There were numerous times that I doubted myself and my abilities but she gently assured me to keep moving forward, as slowly as that might be, and everything would fall into place. We decided the health profession was a good place to start and I chose radiologic technology as a profession.

The academic aspect of school was enjoyable and I did well. However, the clinical aspect I found to be much more difficult and challenging. I struggled to pass in this area. I saw this as a challenge to be met and was committed to completing this program. I did end up with a passing grade in the clinical area of the program.

After seeing Flo for approximately two years and after two years of schooling, I was ready to enter the workforce again. I worked as a radiologic technologist for almost five years and was happy and well adjusted. I worked at St. Clare's hospital in the middle of Hell's Kitchen in Manhattan. It was a very poor neighborhood and many of the patients were afflicted with the AIDS virus. It took me a while (about a year and a half) to learn my trade confidently, but once I did everything fell into place. I even started a co-ed softball team with some fellow workers and we won trophies for second place in our division. We played our games in Central Park, which was a lot of fun.

As Flo told me years earlier, "steps toward a more suitable vocation would arise, that I would be led from there." After three years working as an x-ray technologist, I began looking into other areas of the hospital that I might find more rewarding. I felt physical therapy suited me better, as there was more patient contact.

I began taking prerequisite courses at night toward my master's degree in the field. However, soon after completing these courses I was informed in February of 1998 that there would be layoffs in personnel. The hospital was losing many of its patients to the larger hospitals, and as the last person hired in the department, I was the first person to be let go. Union rules.

I felt a sense of loss even though I was preparing to leave there for PT school the following year. But as is sometimes the case was with my illness, it triggered in me a deep and painful depression that took away fourteen years of my life. I went into it deeply and quickly. As I mentioned previously it was almost unendurable at its worst moments.

Due to its severity and duration, I needed psychiatric help

immediately, though I did not seek out a counselor until several years later. I was simply not able to communicate with another human being in that way at the time.

After my ECT treatments lifted me into a more moderate depression I did start to seek out counseling but I did not "connect" with anyone as I had with Flo. I tried a few psychotherapists, most of whom were nice enough, but they did not have any insight into my illness. It was also difficult to stay with one due to my multiple manic episodes, which sometimes set me back for weeks and months at times.

I finally found Dr. Helen Baietto, who is a knowledgeable, compassionate, and an extremely insightful psychologist. I first went to see her while recovering from a manic episode in June of 2011—thirteen years after my descent into depression.

During my first year with Dr. Baietto, she gained my trust quickly. We first worked on gaining back my stability from this recent bout of mania and afterwards, when the mania was resolved, we worked on managing my more difficult phase of this illness, dealing with my moderate depression.

She was there mostly for support and helped give me insight into this illness. While I had family behind me 100 percent, they did not understand my illness the way that she did, and she was there to listen, understand, and support me. She also encouraged me to do things, not to be so isolated, as many people who are depressed tend to shut themselves off from society.

So, I went about taking on outside challenges. I went through one semester of a physical therapy program at a local community college, though due to my depression I could not complete all of my classes. I also took two anatomy courses that I did complete. I always pushed myself, even if I did not know if I could handle the upcoming challenge, even if I had much self-doubt I persevered through my challenges. I also had some social contact with some of my classmates.

One year after working with Dr. Baietto. I achieved stability and freedom from my depression with a newer mood stabilizer, Abilify. I realized, though, that there was still much work to be done.

After being ill for so many years, I was left, as she described it, "in space." I had been very isolated for several years and had extreme generalized anxiety. The illness had left me without any confidence or enthusiasm.

We set to work on that immediately. I needed ways to lessen my anxiety, raise my confidence, and to believe in myself again.

I took a meditation course that proved to be very helpful in reducing my anxiety. I also took a few yoga classes that were helpful; strengthening me as well as further reducing my anxiety. While I am not currently practicing yoga, its benefits (physiological and psychological) are widely documented. My twin sisters practice yoga regularly.

I practice meditation, mainly deep breathing, and I will discuss its benefits further in the next chapter. Along with yoga and meditation I also took a psychology course to sharpen myself mentally.

I then interned for six months at a couple of hospitals doing radiologic technology work, which raised my confidence a great deal. All the while my anxiety lessened.

It took me five years in total to restore my confidence and enthusiasm, as well as rid myself of the anxiety that at one point had overwhelmed me.

In addition, I continued to exercise. I walked three to four times a week and also lifted cases upon cases, kegs upon kegs, of beer at the beverage store. I was becoming fit physically as well as mentally. All these ingredients contributed to my overall well-being.

I also learned through my therapist to develop compassion for myself, which wasn't the easiest thing for me to do. My attitude was always to move forward, to fight, to get better. Sometimes though, it serves you well to stop and feel the loss and pain you went through before you can come to care about the way you feel toward yourself.

I have to admit my mentality was like a machine at times. I thought I must keep doing something without letting up when sometimes you need to pause, accept where you are and that things take time to develop. My impatience showed up a number of times, but my therapist would always lead me back to having compassion for myself and patience for the process. I was human, she reminded me, not a machine. So, I took all of these lessons and experiences with me and it has led me to a good place now— physically, mentally, emotionally, and spiritually.

## Types of Therapy

Many kinds of therapy exist. There is no "one-size-fits-all" approach. In addition, some therapies have been scientifically tested more than others. Some people may have a treatment plan that includes only one type of therapy. Others receive treatment that includes elements of several different types. The kind of therapy a person receives depends on his or her needs.

Here are some of the most commonly used therapies. However, it does not cover every detail about therapy. Patients should talk to their doctor or a therapist about planning treatment that meets their needs. Cognitive Behavioral Therapy is what I use and interests me most in my daily life.

## Cognitive Behavioral Therapy

Cognitive behavioral therapy (CBT) is a blend of two therapies: cognitive therapy (CT) and behavioral therapy (BT). CT was developed by psychotherapist Aaron Beck, M.D., in the 1960s. CT focuses on a person's thoughts and beliefs, and how they influence a person's mood and actions, and aims to change a person's thinking to be more adaptive and healthy. Behavioral therapy focuses on a person's actions and aims to change unhealthy behavior patterns.

CBT helps a person focus on his or her current problems and how to solve them. Both patient and therapist need to be actively involved in this process. The therapist helps the patient learn how to identify distorted or unhelpful thinking patterns, recognize and change inaccurate beliefs, relate to others in more positive ways, and change behaviors accordingly. CBT can be applied and adapted to treat many specific mental disorders.

## CBT for Depression

Many studies have shown that CBT is a particularly effective treatment for depression, especially minor or moderate depression. Some people with depression may be successfully treated with CBT only. Others may need both CBT and medication. CBT helps people with depression restructure negative thought patterns. Doing so helps people interpret their environment and interactions with others in a positive and realistic way. It may also help a person recognize things that may be contributing to the depression and help him or her change behaviors that may be making the depression worse.

## CBT for Anxiety Disorders

CBT for anxiety disorders aims to help a person develop a more adaptive response to a fear. A CBT therapist may use "exposure" therapy to treat certain anxiety disorders, such as a specific phobia, post-traumatic stress disorder, or obsessive compulsive disorder. Exposure therapy has been found to be effective in treating anxiety-related disorders. It works by helping a person confront a specific fear or memory while in a safe and supportive environment. The main goals of exposure therapy are to help the patient learn that anxiety can lessen over time and give him or her the tools to cope with fear or traumatic memories.

## CBT for bipolar disorder

People with bipolar disorder usually need to take medication, such as a mood stabilizer. But CBT is often used as an added treatment. The medication can help stabilize a person's mood so that he or she is receptive to psychotherapy and can get the most out of it. CBT can help a person cope with bipolar symptoms and learn to recognize when a mood shift is about to occur. CBT also helps a person with bipolar disorder stick with a treatment plan to reduce the chances of relapse.

## Dialectical Behavior Therapy

Dialectical behavior therapy (DBT), a form of CBT, was developed by Dr. Marsha Linehan. At first, it was developed to treat people with suicidal thoughts and actions. It is now also used to treat people with borderline personality disorder (BPD). BPD is an illness in which suicidal thinking and actions are more common.

The term "dialectical" refers to a philosophic exercise in which two opposing views are discussed until a logical blending or balance of the two extremes—the middle way—is found. In keeping with that philosophy, the therapist assures the patient that the patient's behavior and feelings are valid and understandable. At the same time, the therapist coaches the patient to understand that it is his or her personal responsibility to change unhealthy or disruptive behavior.

DBT emphasizes the value of a strong and equal relationship between patient and therapist. The therapist consistently reminds the patient when his or her behavior is unhealthy or disruptive— when boundaries are overstepped—and then teaches the skills needed to better deal with future similar situations. DBT involves both individual and group therapy. Individual sessions are used to teach new skills, while group sessions provide the opportunity to practice these skills.

Research suggests that DBT is an effective treatment for people with BPD. A recent NIMH-funded study found that DBT reduced suicide attempts by half compared to other types of treatment for patients with BPD.

## Interpersonal Therapy

Interpersonal therapy (IPT) is most often used to treat depression or dysthymia (a more persistent but less severe form of depression).

IPT is based on the idea that improving communication patterns and the ways people relate to others will effectively treat depression. IPT helps identify how a person interacts with other people. When a behavior is causing problems, IPT guides the person to change the behavior. IPT explores major issues that may add to a person's depression, such as grief, or times of upheaval or transition. Sometimes IPT is used along with antidepressant medications.

IPT varies depending on the needs of the patient and the relationship between the therapist and patient. Basically, a therapist using IPT helps the patient identify troubling emotions and their triggers. The therapist helps the patient learn to express appropriate emotions in a healthy way. The patient may also examine relationships in his or her past that may have been affected by distorted mood and behavior. Doing so can help the patient learn to be more objective about current relationships.

A variation of IPT, called interpersonal and social rhythm therapy (IPSRT) was developed to treat bipolar disorder. IPSRT combines the basic principles of IPT with behavioral psychoeducation designed to help patients adopt regular daily routines and sleep/wake cycles, stick with medication treatment, and improve relationships.

## Family-focused Therapy

Family-focused therapy (FFT) was developed by Dr. David Miklowitz and Dr. Michael Goldstein for treating bipolar disorder. It was designed with the assumption that a patient's relationship with his or her family is vital to the success of managing the illness. FFT includes family members in therapy sessions in order to improve family relationships, which may support better treatment results.

Therapists trained in FFT work to identify difficulties and conflicts among family members that may be worsening the patient's illness. Therapy is meant to help members find more effective ways to resolve those difficulties. The therapist educates family members about their loved one's disorder, its symptoms and course, and how to help their relative manage it more effectively. When families learn about the disorder, they may be able to spot early signs of a relapse and create an action plan that involves all family members. During therapy, the therapist will help family members recognize when they express unhelpful criticism or hostility toward their relative. The therapist will teach family members how to communicate negative emotions in a better way. Several studies have found FFT to be effective in helping a patient become stable and prevent relapses.

FFT also focuses on the stress family members feel when they care for a relative with bipolar disorder. The therapy aims to prevent family members from "burning out" or disengaging from the effort. The therapist helps the family accept how bipolar disorder can limit their relative. At the same time, the therapist holds the patient responsible for his or her own well-being and actions to a level that is appropriate for the person's age.

- Generally, the family and patient attend sessions together. The needs of each patient and family are different, and those needs determine the exact course of treatment. However, the main components of a structured FFT usually include: Family education on bipolar disorder
- Building communication skills to better deal with stress
- Solving problems together as a family

There is much help out there. If you can find a therapist through a recommendation, that is ideal. If not, see a few on a trial basis. You will know when you have found a therapist that you feel you work well with. Developing trust is key to a successful relationship. If you don't find a good fit at first, try another one. I went through several therapists who were compassionate but didn't have enough knowledge of my illness until I found Dr. Baietto.

"A single, grateful thought towards heaven
is the most complete prayer."
—Gotthold Ephraim Lessing

# CHAPTER 7

## Prayer, Meditation, and Yoga

I achieved stability in 2012, but my work on myself was not yet complete. I didn't know it at the time but my illness, which lasted fourteen years, left me with a great deal of anxiety and no confidence, I needed a way to deal with my anxieties and to rebuild my confidence. Through therapy, holding a steady job, and all of my efforts, it took me five years to quietly build myself up to become a stronger, healthier, and more confident individual. Therapy is imperative while working on stability, as well as after. Three very positive things also helped me with recovery: prayer, meditation, and yoga, with prayer being my most uplifting force.

### Prayer

I always prayed in my writings. "Have faith in God. Have faith in ourselves." This is one statement that I often write down.

I keep in my wallet today a quote from Michelangelo, the great artist and sculptor who said, "Faith in oneself is the best and safest course." While I seek God's counsel on all matters, I ultimately believe all answers to all things come from within. I believe He resides in our hearts as well.

I stopped going to church except for the major holidays, namely Christmas and Easter. I now turned my attention to God in search of guidance; what was I to do now that I had gained stability? My initial intention was simply to go to church, say a few prayers for my family, to those who serve our country, and give thanks for all of my blessings— especially my health and stability. Later on, it was routine for me to go to church at least once or twice a week, to quite simply be silent in the presence of God. I believe in silence God speaks to us and answers our prayers.

When I first entered church after all of those depressed years were finally behind me I knelt down with the intention of giving thanks. However, from somewhere within those four walls, or some place within me, four words resonated throughout my being. They were: love, kindness, compassion, and forgiveness. I didn't question it but I did run home, write it down, and it is how I try to live my life. These four elements were also ingrained in me as I was growing up as a child. Kindness is the essence of love and that is something I have always practiced. Love conquers all. Compassion, I've learned, while directed toward others, one must have compassion for oneself as well. As far as forgiveness is concerned, my interpretation of this is simply to turn those who oppose me and these ideals over to a higher power—God. This is my biggest challenge and something I continuously work on. I must constantly remind myself that He takes care of things that are above and beyond our control.

I believe these four words are the cornerstones to living a good life. Since that time I have not had any new revelations, but I do get a centering for the day when I pray. I think of my life and what I want to do with it—simply, have a steady job, which is imperative and therapeutic for me to help keep my stability, write a book to help others, and continue with the pursuit of education, as this keeps me motivated. I also would like to meet a good, kind, compassionate woman to share my life with. My biggest hopes are for my niece Abby, and for my nephews Dean, Alex, Jack, and Charlie, to find happiness in life. This is my biggest hope and prayer. Finally, that they will live in a more peaceful world.

Norman Vincent Peale gives a guideline of how we can pray and some of its benefits:

1. Set aside a few minutes every day. Do not say anything, simply practice thinking about God. This will make your mind spiritually receptive.

2. Then pray orally, using simple, natural words. Tell God anything that is on your mind. Do not think you must use stereotyped pious phrases. Talk to God in your own language, He understands it.

3. Pray as you go about the business of the day, on the subway, or bus or at your desk. Utilize minute prayers by closing your eyes to shut out the world and concentrating briefly on God's presence. The more you do this every day the nearer you will feel God's presence.

4. Do not always ask when you pray, but instead affirm that God's blessings are being given, and spend most of your prayers giving thanks.

5. Pray with the belief that sincere prayers can reach out and surround your loved ones with God's love and protection.

6. Never use negative thoughts in prayer. Only positive thoughts get result.

7. Always express willingness to accept God's will. Ask for what you want, but be willing to take what God gives you. It may be better than what you ask for.

8. Practice the attitude of putting everything in God's hand. Ask for the ability to do your best and to leave the results confidently to God.

9. Pray for people you do not like or who have mistreated you. Resentment is blockade number one of spiritual power.

10. Make a list of people for whom to pray. The more you pray for the other people, especially those not connected with you, the more prayer results will come back to you.

## Meditation

My experience with meditation consisted of taking a few classes offered at the local adult education program at a nearby high school. I tried a few different meditations but two types of meditation benefitted me most. There is an abundance of videos on meditation that you can get at your local library or bookstore to help you get started or you can take a class as I did Two meditations that I have found helpful and meaningful are :Simply breathing with your awareness on your breath, and Body Scan, which is what I did at the end of my yoga class. I found it extremely relaxing.

If any of them work for you, you can further explore them on your own.

These meditations are from the book, *The Mindful Path through Worry and Rumination* written by Janet H. Kumar, Ph. D.

## A Meditation

Find a comfortable spot that is not too loud or too quiet. Have something to focus your awareness on, your breath, for example.

1) Take deep breaths from your belly
2) Keep your back straight

3) Keep your head, neck and back aligned
4) Your eyes directed straight ahead
5) Tongue gently touching the roof of your mouth
6) Jaws loose
7) Knees below your hips
8) Thumbs gently touching
9) Count your exhalations, one at a time.

Spend fifteen minutes breathing. Try this every morning or evening and see if this helps. Some people get benefits immediately, some it takes more time. But practice, practice, practice.

## Body Scan Meditation

This meditation I've found really helps me to let go of tension, especially in my facial muscles.

Close your eyes. Lie down in a comfortable, quiet place. Take three deep, slow breaths. Extend your exhalation, pushing out the stale air from deep in your lungs.

1) Focus your awareness on the tips of your toes, sensing them relax and get heavier.
2) Next, send your awareness up your feet, ankles, shins, and calves, one at a time. Notice their sensations.
3) Now work your way up your knees, thighs, hips, and pelvis, one by one…bones, flesh, and skin.
4) Now notice your belly rising and falling with each breath. Relax and continue moving along.
5) Bring a feeling of lightness and relaxation to your entire belly and lower back. Breathe and move on.
6) Now bring your awareness to your diaphragm, on top of your belly and then your lungs on top of it, filling up and emptying. Next, focus on your heart, large, warm, and

generous. Visualize the movement of your heart and all of the rich blood pumped through every vessel in your body. Bring your awareness to your ribs and upper back, your spine. Relax your chest and upper back.

7) Now bring your awareness to the tips of your fingers and thumbs, your hands, your wrists, all the bones of your hands and wrists. Next go to the nerves, muscles, and tendons of your forearms, your elbows, your upper arms. Relax them each, one by one.

8) Now move on to your shoulders. Relax this part of your body where your arms, chest, back, and head all connect.

9) Bring your awareness to your neck, your throat, the point at which your neck meets the back of your head, the front of your head.

10) Now go to your chin, jaws, mouth. One by one, be aware of your tongue, teeth, gums, and nose. Sense your cheeks, ears, skin, hair, bones, eyes, and eyelids. Go to your forehead and eyebrows. Relax your brain, your skull, your scalp.

11) Take three deep breaths again. Extend the last exhalation, pushing out the stale air. Open your eyes and turn to your side. Lift yourself up slowly.

Meditation is commonly used for relaxation and stress reduction, and is considered a type of mind-body complementary medicine. It produces a deep state of relaxation and a tranquil mind.

During meditation, you focus your attention and eliminate the stream of jumbled thoughts that may be crowding your mind and causing stress. This process may result in enhanced physical and emotional well-being.

Meditation can give you a sense of calm, peace and balance which benefits both your emotional well-being and your overall health.

And these benefits don't end when your meditation session

ends. Meditation can help carry you more calmly through your day and may improve certain medical conditions.

Meditation teaches you to relate to difficult circumstances and the tensions and emotions they evoke with balance and compassion. It helps you to develop your inner resilience, balance, and strength to take things in stride and come up with creative solutions.

Some benefits of meditation are physiological and some psychological. The physiological benefits are decreased heart rate, lower blood pressure, lowered cholesterol, quicker recovery from stress, enhanced synchronization of the right and left hemispheres of the brain, increased longevity and muscle relaxation.

Psychological benefits include more happiness and peace of mind, greater enjoyment of the present moment, more harmonious relationships, more compassion, and reductions in acute and chronic anxiety.

The goal of mindfulness meditation is to develop the capacity to be fully present for whatever is occurring right here and now. When you're stabilized, your concentration is focused on your breath, you can expand your awareness to include the full range of sensations, both inside and outside, and eventually just welcome whatever presents itself, including thoughts, memories, and emotions.

## Yoga

My yoga experiences were brief yet successful. While I do not currently practice it now, its benefits are widely acknowledged.

I took a great class in the summer of 2012, which was located on the beach in my town. There were about 15 of us, including my sister who urged me to try it. I found this practice to lower my anxiety as well as being physically challenging. The class began at 9 a.m. with the sun still low in the sky and the temperature was generally in the 70s. We had the option of being under the sun and on the sand, which I did though many stayed on the grass under shaded trees. I love being in the sun overlooking the Long Island Sound, which was just a couple hundred feet away from us. There always was a nice breeze off the water. Our instructor, Donna, was a very gentle and knowledgeable woman who had taught yoga for several years. Since this was new to me I found some of the positions like the tree pose to be very challenging and found that I didn't have such great balance. When I attempted Downward facing dog she came to my side and told me I was trying too hard, to be a little gentler, and to breathe. I realized, this wasn't quite as easy as it looked.

I went for the several sessions the course took to complete and at the final session she selected me to do the bridge pose in front of the class. What did leave a lasting impression with me was that each session ended with a guided meditation called body scan. This basically raised your physical awareness from your toes to your torso, then ultimately up to your neck, face, and the top of your head. This completely relaxed me almost to the point of falling asleep. Again, this is my favorite meditation and I recommend to anyone who really wants to let go of tension. A brief description of yoga derived from The Mayo Clinic:

"Yoga is considered a mind-body type of complementary and alternative medicine practice. Yoga brings together physical and mental disciplines to achieve peacefulness of body and mind, helping you relax and manage stress and anxiety.

Yoga has many styles, forms and intensities. Hatha yoga, in particular, may be a good choice for stress management. Hatha is one of the most common styles of yoga, and beginners may like its slower pace and easier movements. But most people can benefit from any style of yoga— it's all about your personal preferences.

The core components of hatha yoga and most general yoga classes are:

- Poses. Yoga poses, also called postures, are a series of movements designed to increase strength and flexibility.

Poses range from lying on the floor while completely relaxed to difficult postures that may have you stretching your physical limits.

- Breathing. Controlling your breathing is an important part of yoga. In yoga, breath signifies your vital energy. Yoga teaches that controlling your breathing can help you control your body and quiet your mind.

The potential health benefits of yoga include: stress reduction, improved fitness, and management of chronic conditions. It definitely helped me a great deal with my anxiety. "It also helps perfect your posture, increases your blood flow, gives you peace of mind, and gives you inner strength."

As you can see through all of the above; prayer, meditation, and yoga all contribute to many aspects of your well-being. I encourage you to give them a try. I initially tried these in helping with my generalized anxiety. Of the three above, prayer works best for me. Every person is unique, thus what works for one person may not work for another. One only knows by trying.

"I'm thankful for the incredible advances in medicine
that have taken place during my lifetime.
I almost certainly wouldn't still be here
if it weren't for them."
—Billy Graham

# CHAPTER 8

## Psychiatrists, Medications, Treatments

Here is an introduction by my psychiatrist Doctor Maria Benetos on treating Bipolar disorder followed by my personal experiences.

In order to properly treat bipolar disorder, one needs to consider addressing both "poles" of the disease: from "above" (the manic episode) and from "below" (the depressed episode). There are specific medications formulated to balance certain brain chemicals, also known as neurotransmitters, to treat and prevent manic, hypomanic, mixed and depressive episodes. They are classified into two categories: mood stabilizers and antipsychotics. Some mood stabilizers include lithium, carbamazepine, valproic acid, and lamotrigine. Lithium, carbamazepine and valproic acid are FDA indicated and effective in treating acute manic episodes. Lamictal is more effective in treating the depressive episodes.

The "atypical" or "second generation" antipsychotics are preferred and several are approved for treatment in bipolar disorder. Some of the atypical antipsychotic medications that have earned an FDA indication for treatment of acute mania include olanzapine, quetiapine, ziprasidone, asenapine, aripiprazole and risperidone. The pharmacotherapy of mania usually requires the combination of a mood stabilizer and an atypical antipsychotic. The atypical antipsychotics are the only class of medications that have proven to be most efficacious in the treatment of bipolar depression. There are three FDA approved medications for bipolar depression, which include lurasidone, olanzapine-fluoxetine (Symbyax), and quetiapine.

Patients who suffer with bipolar disorder will agree that acute mania is easier to treat, less cumbersome and the majority of the illness is occupied by depression. Furthermore, the treatment of mania is less challenging for physicians and patients. There are many effective treatments for mania than there are for depression. It is important to remember some important facts about depression in bipolar disorder. The depressive episodes in bipolar disorder do not respond to the traditional SSRI's and SNRI's that are used to treat depression in major depressive disorder. In fact, these medications can exacerbate the symptoms and worsen the overall course of the disease. Furthermore, SSRI's or SNRI's can trigger a manic episode in those suffering with bipolar depression. The symptoms of depression in bipolar and major depressive disorder are almost indistinguishable which makes the diagnosis of bipolar depression extremely challenging, prolonging patient suffering and the time to achieve recovery. Fortunately, there are some subtle hints that can identify the presence of bipolar depressive illness. There may be a family history of bipolar disorder, substance use disorders, an early onset of depression with high frequency and severity of depressive episodes +/- psychotic features, a history of post-partum depression +/- psychotic features, and a history of poor or adverse responses to traditional antidepressants (SSRI's and SNRI's). It is important to note that an individual may frequently complain of constant or chronic anxiety, irritation, distractibility, restlessness, agitation or impulsivity. It is more often than not that a person with an underlying bipolar disorder could never actually experience a manic episode The sooner a diagnosis of bipolar depression can be made, the appropriate type of medication can be initiated and reduce the duration of the patient's impairment in function and quality of life.

Electroconvulsive therapy or ECT is used predominantly to treat depression in major depressive disorder and bipolar disorder. ECT involves the induction of a seizure in the brain that causes the release of monoamine neurotransmitters and neurohormones and promotes neurogenesis within the brain's structures in order to undo and relieve the negative impact the depression has had on the brain. It has proven to be effective in cases shown to be resistant to improvement after several courses of pharmacotherapy. ECT can also be used to treat acute psychosis in disorders such as schizophrenia. ECT is considered in clinically urgent situations because of the efficacy and speed of its response on patients. It is indicated when a patient is in severe distress and the symptoms are not helped by pharmacological or psychological treatment, there is the risk of imminent suicidality, the presence of psychosis, and/or the patient is unable to maintain adequate life sustaining nutrition and fluid intake.

In the setting of bipolar affective disorder, ECT is considered the first line treatment in severe major depression. ECT is used less frequently to treat hypomania or mania because acutely manic patients frequently respond to pharmacotherapy. ECT may also be effective for medication resistant mixed episodes of bipolar disorder. There is no standard number of treatments required for an acute course of ECT. On average in the United States, the frequency of treatments is 3 times per week and patients usually report being free of symptoms with 6-12 treatments. Many psychiatric medications can be continued during a course of ECT due to the benefits they have with the ongoing treatment. The most common adverse effect of ECT is cognitive impairment and difficulty with remembering recent events but the effects on memory are short lived. ECT is not associated with an increased risk of dementia. Other common adverse effects include headache, nausea, and myalgias. Less common adverse effects include dental and tongue injuries, fractures (in severe osteoporosis) and aspiration pneumonia.

## My Experiences With Psychiatrists

Psychiatrists differ on their level of expertise. Just like any other profession, some are more up to date on the newest level of treatments available, some offer more hope than others, some are more compassionate or attuned to their patients than others. I went in total to about 10 different psychiatrists in my journey for wellness.

What I've found is that the best psychiatrist is one who gives you hope; that there will be a full resolution to your illness. Many times, I have encountered psychiatrists who believe that partial success is good enough and complacent in their attitudes and efforts. But when you find the right one-one who is hopeful, knowledgeable, and what I believe to be a key ingredient is one who is up to date on the newest medications and treatments is the one to stick with.

And so, I searched. I didn't listen to the doctor who threw negative statistics at me. One doctor told me only 1-2% of people with bipolar disorder fully recover and lead productive lives. I did not see him after that. I wanted a doctor to tell me though my case was stubborn, new medications and treatments were coming out all the time.

During the time I was going through my depression, new treatments such as TMS or transcranial magnetic stimulation, was just being researched and was not yet FDA approved for the treatment of depression. Now it is. The medication Abilify, which eventually pulled me all the way out of depression was not introduced until 2003, well after the onset of my depression. And there have been many other medications available and a lot more research is going toward medications and treatments.

A doctor, be it a psychiatrist, psychologist or other mental healthcare worker who is either complacent or doesn't give you hope is a signal that it's time to go on to another one. If you have one recommended to you great, if not as in my experiences, trial and error.

After 4 and ½ years of no success and being labeled as "medication resistant," I finally found a compassionate, informative psychiatrist in Dr. Marianne Hendrix of Smithtown, New York. She told me of a treatment that was available at the time that many people responded to when medications weren't working. This treatment, called Electroconvulsive Therapy or ECT, was effective for many people who were in a similar position as I was. Dr. Hendrix sent me to another doctor to perform these treatments and I went religiously three times a week for one and a half years. While the ECT's did not pull me all the way out of my severe depression, it put me into a more moderate state of depression. I was no longer suffering as I had been. The good news was that medications now had some effect on me but unfortunately due to the bipolar nature of my illness, the anti-depressants prescribed would send me into a manic episode which would last for days, weeks, or months. And every time my mania was resolved I returned to my previously moderate state of depression. After going through several doctors without any success I decided to go back to see Dr. Hendrix to see if there was anything that could be done for my case. She informed me that anti-depressants were not what was prescribed here as she explained that I try a newer mood stabilizer—its name was Abilify. I started at a very low dosage and over the course of a couple of months I was beginning to feel better! Another month and I was stable again—for the first time in fourteen years!

## Nonconventional Treatments

There are a couple of nonconventional or 'add-on' treatments which go in conjunction with medications, conventional treatments, and psychotherapy. Two of these methods are light and pet therapy.

Light therapy (phototherapy) is exposure to light that is brighter than indoor light but not as bright as direct sunlight (ultraviolet light, full spectrum light, heat lamps, and tanning lamps are not used for light therapy).

Light therapy may help with depression, jet lag, and sleep disorders. It may help reset your "biological clock" (circadian rhythms), which control sleeping and waking. People use light therapy to treat seasonal affective disorder (SAD), which is depression related to shorter days and reduced sunlight exposure during the fall and winter months. Most people with SAD feel better after they use light therapy. This may be because light therapy replaces the lost sunlight exposure and resets the body's internal clock.

Light therapy may be most effective when you use it first thing in the morning when you wake up. You and your doctor or therapist can determine when light therapy works best for you. Response to this therapy usually occurs in 2 to 4 days, but it may take up to 3 weeks of light therapy before symptoms of SAD are relieved.

It's not clear how well light therapy works at other times of the day. But some people with SAD (perhaps those who wake up early in the morning) may find it helpful to use light therapy for 1 to 2 hours in the evening, stopping at least 1 hour before bedtime.

Throughout my adolescence, I had a cat named Cloudy. She was the most comforting pet I ever had. She was always there for me during my difficult, and I believe mildly depressed, adolescence. I've learned through experience and reading that pets can relieve depression: they offer a soothing presence, and unconditional love and acceptance. Pets alter our behavior—we calm down when we are with our dogs, cats, and other pets. Pets make us responsible. With pets come great responsibility, and responsibility—according to depression research—promotes mental health.

## Some Side Effects from My Medications

The biggest side effect I had due to the multiple medications I took caused me a weight gain in excess of fifty pounds.

One doctor gave me a thorough checkup and blood work and found that lithium was doing irreparable damage to my kidneys. She sent me to a nephrologist who informed me that I had elevated creatinine levels and I had to immediately discontinue taking the medication or more damage would result.

If you are taking Lithium or any other medication which requires regular blood work it is of utmost important that you follow your doctor's orders as toxicity can develop in some of your major organs like your kidneys as was in my case.

One mood stabilizer caused me nausea and vomiting almost on a daily basis. It became so regular that my psychiatrist referred me to a gastroenterologist who gave me an endoscopy. The medication was indeed the cause. Another medication, I found, that I just couldn't tolerate.

Then there were a couple of medications which caused me involuntary facial muscle twitching. They were ineffective as well so I discontinued their use.

Doctors and patients can work together to find the best medication or medication combination, and dose.

I feel it is important here to let you know of some current medications, treatments, and their side effects: however, go to the NIMH website and to your doctor for the most up to date medications and treatments.

There is much hope for the future. While it may or may not happen in my lifetime, there is much hope for future generations with many illnesses, that there will be cures so they will not have to go through the trials and suffering of those before them.

"In the garden of literature,
the highest and the most charismatic flowers
are always the quotations."
—Mehmet Murat Ildan

# CHAPTER 9

## Inspiring Quotations

"You can't keep a good man (or woman) down."
—Bob Corbin

"Faith in oneself is the best and safest course."
—Michaelangelo

"Faith is a sounder guide than reason.
Faith has no limits."
—Blaine Pascal

"Three things in human life are important:
the first is to be kind; the second is to be kind;
and the third is to be kind."
—Henry James

"Praying makes me happy."
—My ninety-seven-year-old great aunt,
Vincenza. We affectionately call her Zia.

"With God all things are possible."
—Jesus

"When in doubt keep going,
you're bound to stumble on to something."
—Charles Kettering

"Be kind for everyone you meet is fighting a hard battle."
—Plato

"Nothing great can be accomplished without enthusiasm."
—Emerson

"Folks are about as happy as they make up their minds to be."
—Abe Lincoln

"Love conquers all."
—Virgil

"To make the best of, the most of, today each day."
—Mary Stangarone (my mother)

"To face despair and not give in to it, that's courage."
—Ted Koppel

"Confidence that one is of value and significance as a unique individual is one of the most precious possessions which anyone can have."
—Anthony Starr

"All high beauty has a moral element in it."
—Ralph Waldo Emerson

"If we are motivated by love in its highest sense, we will act better than if differently motivated. We have the ability to choose a spiritual life over a carnal one, thereby pointing out the direction of our choices."

"Living well and beautifully and justly are all one thing."
—Socrates

"Not only is there a right to be happy, there is a duty to be happy. So much sadness exists in the world that we are all under obligation to contribute as much joy as lies within our powers."
—John Sutherland Bonell

"Walk boldly and wisely. There is a hand above you that will help you on."
—Philip James Bailey

"Trust in the Lord with all your heart. In all the ways acknowledge Him, and He shall direct your path."

"That man is happiest who lives from day to day, and asks no more, garnering the simple goodness of a life."
—Euripides

"We must give ourselves more earnestly and intelligently and generously than we have to the happy duty of appreciation."

—Mariana Griswold Van Rensselaer

"Faith sees the invisible, believes the incredible (miracles big and small), and receives the impossible."

"Life is not easy for any of us. But what of that? We must have perseverance and above all confidence in ourselves. We must believe that we are gifted for something, and that thing, at whatever cost, must be attained."

—Marie Curie

"If the only prayer you say in your whole life is "Thank you," that would suffice".

—Meister Eckhart

"To be simple is to be great."

—Ralph Waldo Emerson

"With ordinary talent and extraordinary perseverance, all things are attainable."

—Sir Thomas Foxwell Buxton

"Whatever course you decide upon, there is always someone to tell you that you are wrong. There are always difficulties arising which tempt you to believe that your critics are right. To map out a course of action and follow it to an end requires....courage."

—Ralph Waldo Emerson.

"Before you begin a thing remind yourself that difficulties and delays quite impossible to foresee are ahead…you can only see one thing clearly, and that is your goal. Form a mental vision of that and cling to it through thick and thin."

—Kathleen Norris

"The essence of love is kindness."

—Robert Louis Stevenson

"Gratitude is the sign of noble souls."

—Aesop

"Without the assistance of the Divine Being…I cannot succeed. With that assistance, I cannot fail."

—Abraham Lincoln

"Follow your own way of speaking to our Lord sincerely, lovingly, confidently, and simply, as your heart dictates."

—Jane Frances De Chantal

"Our thanks to God should always precede our requests."

—Anonymous

"Who rises from prayer a better man, his prayer is answered."

—George Meredith

"One's self-image is very important because if that's in good shape, then you can do anything or practically anything."

—Sir John Gielgud

"Measure yourself by your best moments, not by your worst. We are too prone to judge ourselves by the moments of despondency and depression."

—Robert Johnson

"A life of reaction is a life of slavery, intellectually and spiritually. One must fight for a life of action, not reaction."

—Rita Mae Brown

"Any man's life will be filled with constant and unexpected encouragement if he makes up his mind to do his level best each day."

—Booker T. Washington

"Great thoughts always come from the heart."

—Vauvenargues

"A hard beginning makes a good ending."

—John Heywood

"Self-trust is the first key to success."

—Ralph Waldo Emerson

"Character cannot be developed in ease and quiet. Only through experience of trial and suffering can the soul be strengthened, vision cleared, ambition inspired, and success achieved."

—Helen Keller

"Patient endurance attains all things."

—Teresa of Avila

"Success is peace of mind, which is a direct result of knowing you did your best to become the best you are capable of being."

—John Wooden

"Although the world is full of suffering, it is also full of the overcoming of it."

—Helen Keller

Bel a Bel.

—From an Italian dialect in the region where my family was born meaning a nice and easy approach to life which gently was repeated over and over to me and my siblings by my grandparents

"We conquer by continuing."
—George Matheson

# CHAPTER 10

## A Final Thought

I am very fortunate. Though I became my own advocate, I also had the support of my family, in so many ways, through all of my trials. I am most thankful for them and their tremendous support. Second, a great deal of gratitude to my doctors and therapists, who were instrumental in the restoration of my mind, my confidence, my strength, and my overall health. I appreciate my health and renewed sense of self each day.

My objective when I set out to write this book was to reach one person out there suffering with depression or bipolar disorder, and help them to persevere until a resolution is reached; that they find peace, health, strength, and happiness, then my goal would be accomplished.

I was given much inspiration and hope through books, and my hope is that I've given you a good deal of inspiration and hope.

I must admit I feel like I've climbed more than one mountain—and that is a good thing. Battling this illness was without question the hardest thing I've had to do. But with great effort, support, and patience I did it.

Though your case may be stubborn, modern science is coming up with new medications all the time and they will continue to do so. I believe eventually there will be a cure to mental illness but in the meantime, keep pursuing all avenues of treatments. The main thought that arose in me most during the fourteen-year battle with my illness was, "Don't give up; don't ever give up!" This led me to persevere to another day, eventually a brighter day. And remember, "Where's a will, there's a way and where there is no way God will find a way!"

Best wishes on your recovery!

Maximillian Stangarone
maxny@msn.com

# CHAPTER 11

# Resources

National Mental Health Organizations Emergency Contact Numbers

If you feel you are in a crisis due to your depression, call the National Hotline at 1 800 273 5255. If this is an emergency, call 911, or call your health-care provider, or go to your nearest emergency room.

## National Mental Health Organizations:

1) National Alliance on Mental Illness 1 800 950 6264.
   If emergency, call 1 800 543 3638, or www.nami.org
2) National Institute on Mental Health 1 866 615 6464, or www. Nimh.nih.gov

3) Depression and Bipolar Support Alliance
1 800 826 3632, or www. Dbsalliance.org,
if emergency, call 1800 273 talk
4) Mayo Clinic
Mayoclinic.org or call 480-301-8000

BOOKS ARE THE QUIETEST OF FRIENDS,
THEY ARE THE MOST ACCESSIBLE
AND WISEST OF COUNSELORS,
AND THE MOST PATIENT OF TEACHERS.
—Charles William Elliot

# Books That Were Helpful Along the Way

A few inspirational books I have read over the last several years:

The Gifts of Jimmy V – Bob Valvano
Win the Battle – Bob Olson
Anatomy of an Illness – Norman Cousins
The Power of Positive Thinking – Norman Vincent Peale
Enthusiasm Makes the Difference – Norman Vincent Peale
The Tough-Minded Optimist – Norman Vincent Peale
The Essential Vince Lombardi – Vince Lombardi, Jr.
Bird by Bird – Ann Lamott
Writing Through the Darkness – Elizabeth Maynard
The Right to Write – Julia Cameron
Darkness Visible – William Styron
The Little Engine That Could – Watty Piper
Sly Moves – Sylvester Stallone

## Movies that inspired me:

Rocky
The Silver Linings Playbook

# Acknowledgements

This book would not have been possible without my family. Beginning with my parents Vito and Mary Stangarone without whose sacrifice, selflessness, and unfailing support through my most difficult times enabled me to see doctors regularly, put food on the table every day, and did not judge me, I would not be here. Sadly, my father passed away during the writing of this book. Second, to my siblings Burt, Connie, Angela, Susanne, and Martin who, without their love and support I most certainly would not be here today. Jodi, Robert, and Greg who took me to doctor appointments I am grateful for. To my Uncle Frank who typed up my initial edits and was a role model for me throughout my life I am truly thankful. Two psychiatrists who helped me most: Dr. Marianne Hendrix who probably single-handedly saved my life twice and Dr. Maria Benetos a one in a million doctor who combined her mental intelligence with an emotional intelligence and belief in my book instilled a confidence within myself. To Dr. Helen Baietto, who helped me to gain confidence after stabilization with my medication. To my editor, Elizabeth Szaluta who made the book more polished and professional which further instilled a confidence that this book will help others who suffer from mental illness I am truly grateful. One final mention. Had it not been for Saint James Beverage and working with my brother at his store I believe this along with medication was my biggest reason for reclaiming my health so a sincere thank you to my brother Martin!

Printed in the United States
By Bookmasters